BRIGHT

WASHINGTON SQUARE
BY
HENRY JAMES

Intelligent Education

Nashville, Tennessee

BRIGHT NOTES: Washington Square

www.BrightNotes.com

ISBN: 978-1-645422-00-6 (Paperback)

ISBN: 978-1-645422-01-3 (eBook)

Published in accordance with the U.S. Copyright Office Orphan Works and Mass Digitization report of the register of copyrights, June 2015.

Originally published by Monarch Press.

Ralph A. Ranald, 1965

2020 Edition published by Influence Publishers.

Interior design by Lapiz Digital Services. Cover Design by Thinkpen Designs.

Printed in the United States of America.

Library of Congress Cataloging-in-Publication Data forthcoming.

Names: Intelligent Education

Title: BRIGHT NOTES: Washington Square

Subject: STU004000 STUDY AIDS / Book Notes

CONTENTS

HENRY JAMES

. . . .

LIFE (1843 - 1916)

Henry James is probably the outstanding American novelist and stylist. If he is not alone in that rank, he is accompanied by only three or four others, such as Hawthorne, Melville, Twain, and perhaps Faulkner. Even among those, who represent the best in American literature so far as novelists are concerned, James does seem to stand out if only on the basis of his prodigious lifetime of writing. James's writing career extended from the late 1860s to the first two decades of the present century, and he was without question the first American novelist to truly bring his work into the mainstream of world literature. This is not to say that there were not great works in American literature before James's major novels, but it is to say that James made the American novel something more than the product of an American. He made it an art form, a work as sophisticated as the well-written poem, and his works rank with the outstanding writers not only of America, but also of Europe.

The facts of James's life are best seen in relation to his work, for James lived a quiet life and devoted himself to literature as a profession and as a way of life. The following is a brief summary of some of the important dates, but the next section ("Periods in James's fiction") views James's works as the primary material for understanding him. The student should know at least the following: Henry James was born on April 15, 1843, in a house on Washington Square in New York City. James in his autobiography later told of the impressions he had of life because of the humanity he would observe in that respectable section of the great city. Henry's father, Henry James, Senior, was a well-known figure in intellectual circles. He had inherited his wealth and spent much of his time in cultured activity. The novelist's older brother, William, became famous as a philosopher, psychologist, and professor at Harvard University, and the brothers remained close, as their correspondence shows, throughout their lifetimes. Henry James, Senior, believed that his children should be exposed to the culture and life of Europe as a basic part of their life, so he took his sons there when Henry was still an infant. On their return from their first trip, they lived in New York again, but also stayed in Albany. In 1855 they returned to Europe again for three more years of education, some in school, some at the direction of tutors, and some led by the father, in Geneva, London, and Paris. During 1858-1859 the family stayed in Newport, Rhode Island, a very fashionable resort at that time, where Henry and William studied painting with John LaFarge, a well-known artist. In 1859-1860, however, they were in Europe again, this time in Geneva and also Bonn, Germany. In 1862, James entered the Law School at Harvard, while William entered the scientific school at the same university. In that same year, Henry sustained some mysterious injury to his back that kept him out of the Civil War. Around 1865 James began publishing his sketches, critical reviews, and stories, in such magazines as the famous *Atlantic Monthly* and the *North American Review*. It was just a year before this time that the young Henry James had decided on writing as his profession. The student should understand that James's decision was not an idealistic, romantic outburst, but a reasoned and mature commitment to writing as a career. In 1869 James went to Europe, and although he returned to America on several occasions, one can say that from that year on James was a resident of the European continent. Most students of American literature see James's expatriation as a pilgrimage in reverse of the normal pattern; it was a move, one must understand, made by an artist in order to give himself the proper perspective from which he could continue with his craft. James lived for the most part in London, but he spent some time in Paris, Rome, and other European cities. In 1915, although he was unmistakably an American in thought and art, James became a British subject in protest of American neutrality during that time of the First World War. James died in February, 1916.

PERIODS IN JAMES'S FICTION

Much more complete a view of James as a writer comes from looking at the stages in his long and fruitful writing career. F. W. Dupee in *Henry James* breaks that career into the following periods:

1. 1870s: This is James's idealistic phase. He is learning his craft and developing his themes. The works are really not complicated and characters are clearly drawn without too much ambiguity or complexity. Still James achieved in this early period some of his most memorable characters, such as Christopher Newman in *The American* (1877) and Isabel Archer in *The Portrait of a Lady* (1881). Other important early works are *Daisy Miller*, 1879; *The Europeans*, 1878; and *Washington Square*, 1881.

2. 1880s: James in this period became more realistic. He began to deal with more complicated matters such as social institutions and political issues. Some important works are *The Princess Casamassima*, 1885; *The Bostonians*, 1886; and *The Tragic Muse*, 1887.

3. Late 1880s and Early 1890s: At this point, James turned to writing for the theatre with noticeably bad luck. He was humiliated on the night of the opening of his play *Gum Domville*, when the audience was vile to him. An interesting note is that a young critic, George Bernard Shaw, was at that performance.

4. 1890s: During this time James started tackling the problem of evil-evil in the sense of strong characters and their relationship to innocent victims. It was during this period, because James was constantly experimenting in the desire to develop his technique, that the reputation of James as a difficult writer arose. His longer, more complicated sentences became his standard type of writing in this period. The important works are "The Pupil," 1891; *What Maisie Knew*, 1897; and *The Turn of the Screw*, 1898.

5. 1900s: F. O. Matthiessen, a critic, gave this first decade of the twentieth century the name "The Major Phase," and the title is apt. James in this period, with an enormous burst of energy, wrote three major novels: *The Ambassadors*, 1903, but completed in 1901; *The Wings of the Dove*, 1902; and *The Golden Bowl*, 1904. These are James's maturest efforts; they are complex, massive, and difficult novels, but they are among the best in our language. It was during this period that James began editing his own novels and writing his "Prefaces," which

are essays on the problems in writing his works and studies of the novel as art, for the New York Edition of his works.

6. Final Phase: James left two unfinished works at his death: *The Sense of the Past*, 1917; *The Ivory Tower*, 1917.

MAJOR THEMES IN JAMES'S FICTION

Like all writers, James is concerned with the human situation; he is interpreting characters and life. When one refers to the major **themes** of a particular writer, he is thinking of those subjects and preoccupations that persist in a writer, that appear in many, if not most, of his works. The critic R. P. Blackmur, in *The Literary History of the United States*, distinguishes three **themes** in James's fiction: "international theme," the **theme** of the artist in conflict with society, and "the theme of the pilgrim in search of society." One can see that society is basic to James's works; he is constantly evaluating what one society maintains as its values and how these values affect groups and individuals. Many times he contrasts that particular society with the activities and mores of another society. Basically, the two societies that persist in his works are those of America and Europe.

Two dominant images emerge, therefore, in the fiction:

THE INNOCENT

James usually poses an innocent figure. The person is not stupid, not unintelligent. What James means in an innocent person is one who has not been touched by deep experience in worldly matters. These innocents are eager for life and they usually see

5

life in others as an object for their own desires. Usually, in a James novel, these intelligent and eager creatures are corrupted and spoiled by the sophisticated ones in whom the innocents think that the virtues they would like reside. The innocents are candid, and human. They have strength and respond with deep conviction when they see their ideals corrupted. They are almost always intelligent, and they naturally, without affectation, understand good and evil, right and wrong. The sophisticated ones prey on these innocents, because they substitute experience in the world for natural decency. However, the successes of the experienced are hollow. The strong figures in James are the natural good ones.

THE INTERNATIONAL THEME

Most of the things said about the heroes and heroines of a Jamesian work apply to this basic **theme** that James mastered and matured. The international subject is the study of the American abroad. These Americans are unaware of the **conventions** and formalities of Europe; they make mistakes, they have deficiencies in tact and polish, but they have freedom, innocence, and grace, and these more than make up for their lack of experience. James contrasts the two societies very carefully: the American is not yet matured and he is awkward because he does not know how the society he is in expresses itself. He knows that there are deeper and lasting values in the society of Europe, but his natural way is usually in conflict with these values. Europe, on the other hand, does not have the vitality and youthfulness of the American world. Europe is a matter of **convention**, that is, formal responses in social situations. Every move, every act, is deliberate and committed in an established way. In James's last works, Europe does seem to represent an ideal, but the innocent, vital American remains a serious threat to the established order.

If one will examine in the following pages Henry James's *Daisy Miller*, he will see one of James's earliest examinations of the international **theme**. It is surprisingly a very full look at the whole subject in its basic forms. *Daisy Miller* looks forward to *The Portrait of a Lady* and the great accomplishment in the character of Isabel Archer and also to *The Wings of the Dove* and the more complete and subtle characterization of Milly Theale. These later works are more complicated, more difficult in style, but *Daisy Miller* presents the essential ideas inherent in the international theme.

Daisy, as a character, is an innocent, but the whole problem of innocence, especially in contrast to the influence of evil, comes out most vividly in *The Turn of the Screw*. There the entire story examines the potential meanings, the ironies and ambiguities, of this basic **theme**. Together *The Turn of the Screw* and *Daisy Miller* are two of Henry James's most popular stories. They contain his essential **themes** and his essential style. They are a good place for all students of James to begin.

THE JAMESIAN NOVEL

Henry James looked upon the novel as a work of art. In the truest sense of the word art, one can say James was one of the first writers to think of the novel in this way. James did not use the novel as a social document or as a forum for his philosophy. To James, the novel is a form complete in itself. Admittedly, he is difficult to read. The following is a synopsis of what one can expect to find in his works: First, a Jamesian novel is not a vehicle for something else. The story, plot, dialogue are complete within the work itself. Second, in a James novel, there is always what James referred to as the "central consciousness," that is, a mind and person through whom the story is being presented to the reader. James is always conscious of how the reader is hearing and seeing his story. Basically, he stays away from the omniscient narrator except for occasional comments. The omniscient narrator means that the story is told from the point of view of the author. He knows all the characters and what they are thinking and doing. James usually attempts to tell the story from the point of view of a character in the work. In *The Turn of the Screw*, James tells the story from the point of view of the first person narrator. In *Daisy Miller*, the story is seen through the mind of Winterbourne. The reader can note there that the story is never seen from Daisy's point of view. The story is about how Daisy is seen by others, especially Winterbourne. The reader should understand that James's dominating technical device is point of view, the decision that the author had made on from whose eyes, ears, and mind he is going to tell the story to the reader. Third, the reader soon realizes that in James's novels there are rarely, if ever, plain ornaments. Dialogue is never just plain talk; it is always moving the plot forward. Description always establishes a scene so that one can understand the direction of the work. Scenes are always full of meaning in relation to other things in the novel. Fourth, one can summarize all the above by saying that a Jamesian novel is always organic, all things are in relation to the whole. Nothing, not character, plot, story, scene, dialogue, description-nothing is isolated. All parts are related.

JAMES'S CRITICISM ON THE NOVEL

During his writing career James wrote many reviews, essays, and articles on writers and their works, but he made an outstanding contribution to the study of the novel in two separate parts of critical writings. First, from 1907 to 1917 there was issued a collected edition of Henry James's works. Usually this edition is referred to as "The New York Edition" by James scholars. For this collection, James selected the works, chose to leave some of his less successful works out (although some of these, such as *The Bostonians*, are considered highly now), revised passages in the works, and for each volume wrote a critical preface. These prefaces contain some of the most sophisticated discussions of the art of the novel in all literature. Usually, in each preface James tried to explain how he came upon the story, what he referred to as the "germ." Then James explained what possibilities he saw in the germ and the problems he was confronted with in developing the novel. In many cases James pointed to outstanding devices, techniques, and in many other cases James pointed out some of the mistakes he felt he had made. There are further discussions of the prefaces to *The Turn of the Screw* and *Daisy Miller*. These essays are surely among the most important documents on prose fiction, for they give an insight not only into the mind of a great writer, they also reveal the art of the novel.

Second, in September, 1884, James published in *Longman's*, a magazine, an essay known as "The Art of Fiction." It was written in reply to a lecture given by a Walter Besant, a Victorian novelist and historian. Besant's lecture, "Fiction as a Fine Art," has been forgotten except by literary scholars, but James's essay has remained one of the most important studies on the art of fiction. One must realize that James was a forerunner of the present thought that the novel can be looked upon as a serious work of art. Some of the more important aspects of the essay are as follows: 1. "The only reason for the existence of a novel is that it does attempt to represent life." He goes on to say that the "novel is history." 2. "The only obligation to which in advance we may hold a novel ... is that it be interesting." James then adds that the ways to make a novel interesting are innumerable. 3. "A novel is in its broadest definition a personal, a direct impression of life: that, to begin with, constitutes its value, which is greater or less according to the intensity of the impression." 4. James agrees that a novel cannot be written without a deep sense of reality, but the reality must come from an awareness of the extent of experience. In a famous **metaphor** James explains experience: "Experience is never limited ... ; it is an immense sensibility, a kind of huge spider-web of the finest silken threads suspended in the chamber of the consciousness, and catching every airborne particle in its tissue." 5. James refers to the novel as a "living thing." In other words, it is organic. (See under the Jamesian novel.) 6. According to James, there can be no distinction between character and incident. These are complements of each other. 7. Finally, James states one of the most quoted critical ideas in the essay: "We must grant the artist his subject, his idea, his donnee: our criticism is applied only to what he makes of it." There are many other items in both the "Art of Fiction" and the "Prefaces," but the student should be aware that most of the modern terms we use about the novel, the criticism that we apply to the novel, the serious manner in which we view the novel - these and other ideas had their most serious first statement in the criticism of Henry James.

WASHINGTON SQUARE

. . . .

A BRIEF INTRODUCTORY NOTE

As F. O. Matthiessen said, in his important book *Henry James: The Major Phase*, we can understand James's philosophy of life "only by apprehending the pattern of his work as a whole." It is dangerous to take isolated speeches, even of important characters such as Newman or Strether, for the complete statement of James's morality. Still, if one looks over a representative body of James's fiction, the ideal which may be stated as "a rich life freely lived" becomes apparent, and while most of his characters fall short of the attainment of this highest good, it is constantly present in James's consciousness. Above all, a rich life is not to be attained by looting the emotional resources, the vitality, the "life" of others, for such goods, like blood-money or the proceeds of slavery, do not profit the receivers thereof, as James's wisest characters perceive.

It is the specific application of this doctrine to *Washington Square* which leads to our heightened awareness of the meaning of that work, which carries it beyond the limits of what might constitute simply "a good story." The four major characters

- if Mrs. Penniman can be regarded as major - all have their impacts on the personality and consciousness of Catherine. Mrs. Penniman is merely silly, but she is the victim of an idea: it might be called the idea of being in love with love, and wishing unconsciously to live this interest vicariously in the person of Catherine. This is the least offense; the entrapment of a shallow person by a naive and shallow and sentimental idea. Still, Mrs. Penniman does harm to Catherine.

At another level is the victimization of Morris Townsend. Living in some vague kind of hope that he will be able to marry Catherine, he does not put forth the kind of effort which his situation demands, and does not make a place for himself in the active world, though he has the ability; even the Doctor admits that. He is victimized by a prospect, never realized. But worst of all, in terms of the damage he does, is Dr. Sloper - and in the detailed analysis and commentary upon *Washington Square*, one can see how the Doctor, outwardly a devoted and prudent father, ruins his daughter's life.

Washington Square appeared in 1880, which places it relatively early in James's creative career. It can be read for pleasure, as R. P. Blackmur and other Jamesian critics have pointed out-it can be read simply as a slice of life from a rather cultured though narrow upper-middle-class stratum of mid-nineteenth-century New York society. It has been translated into many languages, and like such a work as Arthur Miller's play *Death of a Salesman*, written three quarters of a century later, it has evidently been taken to symbolize certain things about America including some which the authors concerned never intended or even dreamed of.

But it is a good story above all, if on the surface a rather quiet and subdued one. On deeper levels, it is a story of spiritual violence; a case history of a psychological trauma inflicted on a rather defenseless and innocent girl by a selfish father and an equally selfish and shallow would-be suitor or lover. The **theme** of the story, indeed, involves one of the Jamesian cardinal sins, as described in more detail in the section above on Jamesian morality; the violation of sovereign human personality, and the regarding of a human being as an object, a thing, rather than something inalienable, free, and worthy of respect.

Catherine Sloper, the girl who is the central figure of *Washington Square*, is such a victimized human being as one often sees throughout the novels and short stories of Henry James. James, it will be remembered by those familiar with the incidental facts of his biography, studied law at Harvard Law School for over a year during 1862 - 3. He was probably temperamentally unsuited to the practice of law, as he himself realized - though he did pick up some of the lawyer's talents of sharp observation of detail, or at least this quality was intensified in him. But what he disliked about the law as a social instrument was its crudity. It was, for him, a blunt instrument, quite incapable of directing or prescribing real civilization and culture. The law proposes, among other things, to keep people from being victimized. But it can only act on a crude physical level. If one person assaults, wounds, or kills another physically, one is punished physically by the law, which represents the organized and codified will of society.

But how can one measure the kind of damage which is done to the Catherine Slopers of this world? How is the damage done? As R. P. Blackmur wrote, in his "Introduction" to the Dell Laurel edition of this novel (July, 1959), Catherine Sloper has been "progressively tampered with." She has been tampered with by the two men in the story, her father and her lover - but finally, and most disastrously for her own integrity of personality, tampered with by herself, in that her reaction to the murky emotional situation in which she is involved is to become disoriented from society and from normal life. This is what the plot of *Washington Square* is "about."

The central figures in *Washington Square* are three: Catherine Sloper, her father, Dr. Austin Sloper, and her lover, Morris Townsend. The plot is thus generated by a triangular conflict among three people who have aims which are ultimately irreconcilable. And in this conflict, none the less violent for being mental and emotional rather than physical, the person who is the most innocent, Catherine, suffers and is damaged the most. We have the feeling, upon our concluding the reading of *Washington Square*, that what becomes of Morris Townsend is of little importance because of the way he has conducted himself towards Catherine and because of his basic weakness. But something has so affected Catherine's emotional life- her spirit, it may be - that she will be henceforth incapable of leading a normal life. She has been violated, though not at all in the physical sense, for this, like most of James's stories and novels, operates on the moral and psychological levels, not the physical.

This is all by way of explaining why superficially nothing seems to happen in the story. The psychological action is violent, if by violence one means some disproportionate power or force which does injury to human beings-injury, whether deserved or undeserved. To return briefly to the point about Henry James's study of the law and his view of it-James does not see Justice as triumphing in life. Very often, the result of human relations is ambiguous, not just, and novels which have an ending reflective of "poetic justice," or perhaps what James's friend and contemporary William Dean Howells called "smiling realism," are not the novels or stories which James cared to write, because he did not consider them a true picture of reality and of the way in which human life is actually lived. And as James always strove to represent "life," in an actual and not a superficial sense, he embodied in *Washington Square* what he thought would actually happen, given the situation, rather than what he would have liked to have happen, or what his readers might have preferred to have happen.

In others of James's novels and stories, Injustice rather than Justice seems to be triumphant. Very often the central character, as for example Christopher Newman in *The American* or Isabel Archer in *The Portrait of A Lady* is called upon to make a far-reaching renunciation in conformity with a higher moral imperative. Renunciation, in fact, is one of the basic modes of approaching life taken by many of James's central characters. And renunciation implies frustration of one's natural destiny. Whether there is renunciation in *Washington Square* remains to be seen in our discussion which follows. But certainly there is frustration, and there is victimization of one human being by another at a level which in James's view was an offense against Life itself. The precise nature of that offense and its outcome will be examined as we progress through the detailed commentary on this intriguing short novel or novelette.

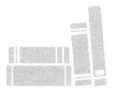

WASHINGTON SQUARE

SECTIONS 1 - 6

. . . .

The structure and format of *Washington Square* in part have their origins undoubtedly from the book's original publication in serial form. It was published in *Cornhill Magazine* and in *Harper's New Monthly Magazine* during July-November, 1880, republished in book form in Boston later that same year, and has since been published in a number of editions, including the Dell Laurel paperback edition [1959] which also includes the novelette *The Europeans.*

The novel, as published in book form, is divided into thirty-five numbered sections, and the most satisfactory form of the present analysis and commentary seems to be simply to take up each one of these numbered sections in turn. The use of the device of numbered sections is related, of course, to the original serial publication of the book-in order to sustain reader interest in a serialized magazine story, it is necessary for a writer to make use of what might be called sub-climaxes, or points in the action of the story which would serve as logical stopping points for a reader engrossed in a magazine story, and would lead him to wish to purchase the next issue. The whole subject of serial publication of James's works could lead to a special study, for which the present commentary has no space, but readers should at least be aware of these facts, because of their influence on the fictional forms and methods exemplified in such a work as *Washington Square*. The individual numbered sections of the thirty-five composing this novel in turn form certain natural groupings, and the basis and manner of such groupings will be discussed here.

SECTION I

The scene is set in New York in the first half of the nineteenth century. It is an upper-class, or upper-middle class, segment of New York society, in which Dr. Austin Sloper lives and has his medical practice, for as a distinguished and able physician in that society, he can command both large fees and enormous social respect. As James says, he is respected as an honest man, and at the time during which the action of the story takes place, he is about fifty years of age-what he has, he has obtained by his own industry and success in his profession.

Evidently Dr. Austin Sloper had been married, in the year 1820 when he was aged 27, to a Miss Catherine Harrington, who had given him with her hand a substantial dowry, as was the expectation of a young husband of certain social classes in those days. The question of a dowry will play an important part in the marriage, or possible marriage, of Dr. Sloper's daughter, and James may have perhaps raised it from the beginning for this reason. In fact, Dr. Sloper's wife was not only well-off but wealthy. Yet while Dr. Sloper was able to cure many, he could not save two of the most important people: his first child, a son who died aged three, and even more tragically, his own wife, who died in childbed giving birth to their daughter two years after the death of the boy.

"To learn something interesting, and to do something useful ..." is Dr. Sloper's pattern or plan for his life, and James makes it clear that he is, at least in his surface qualities, quite admirable in his dependability and willingness to expend effort in his profession. He has been his own severest judge, and this was especially true upon the death of his wife, for the Doctor blamed himself for this, though given the quality of medicine prior to the twentieth century in the Western world, there was probably nothing he or any other physician could have done to save Mrs. Sloper. As the first Section concludes, we are informed that Dr. Sloper really considers his daughter a sort of consolation prize; a second best, leading him to think that she, unlike her mother, would never be lost to him, because the hand of Fate or Chance, or whatever had taken his wife from him, would not take his much plainer daughter.

Comment

In this Section, something of the character of Dr. Sloper is begun to be established. One must be careful, in terms of James's theory of the writing of fiction, of using too much direct narrative to set the background of a novel. The "**exposition**" (a dramatic term: the beginning of a play which begins in the midst of things and shows in action what has gone before) of a James novel or story tends to follow the dramatic practice, for James himself was a dramatist, although hardly as successfully as he was a writer of fiction. Thus, he cuts his sheer description of Dr. Sloper and his history to a bare minimum in the first Section, for he wishes Dr. Sloper to show what manner of man he is by his actions and his sayings, rather than by description and narration. As Section I ends, we have an impression, just an impression, of the Doctor as being a precise man who, while he has many admirable qualities, especially as related to his noble profession of healing the sick, is rather too cold and self-contained, too demanding of himself and therefore too demanding of others. And we seem to find hints of a possible strain in the relationship between Dr. Sloper and his daughter, even at this early stage in the story.

SECTION II

A large amount of life is quickly passed over by James as he develops the background of his story further. The reader already has the notion that Catherine Sloper, while a healthy child, does not really please her father, mainly for accidental reasons. The story narrative leaps and lingers, passing over the first ten years of Catherine Sloper's life. At age ten, Catherine is joined by an addition to the household, Dr. Sloper's widowed sister, Mrs. Penniman, who originally comes to live "temporarily" in the Sloper household at Washington Square. She is the Doctor's elder sister, a woman who had married a poor clergyman and then been left a widow at thirty-three, without anything: children, fortune, or even particularly happy memories. Her name is Lavinia, and it is made clear that the Doctor prefers his younger sister, Mrs. Almond, who is well and happily married, to Mrs. Penniman. But for reasons of convenience, it turns out that the "temporary" arrangement whereby Mrs. Penniman will be a guest in her brother's house, turns into a permanent situation. Ten years after her arrival, when Catherine Sloper is twenty, Mrs. Penniman is still in the house. Apparently, Mrs. Penniman is of a rather romantic disposition, and this is evidenced by the unwise (from her brother's point of view) marriage she had made, which brought her no worldly advantages. The Doctor surmises, that she may inflict her romantic notions upon his daughter, but keeps his eye on the situation.

The Doctor has made up his mind that Catherine is "not clever." He believes in cleverness; that one is good for nothing unless he or she has this quality. Mrs. Penniman, on the other hand, raises the question whether it is better to be clever than to be good. Between the two of them, they discuss and indeed lay out the girl's future. Apparently it is objectively true that Catherine Sloper is not clever, nor is she a great beauty like her mother; she is rather docile and has a pleasant, but in no way an unusual, personality. This is part of the difficulty: the Doctor wishes that his daughter would manifest some unusual or outstanding quality, whether of intelligence, beauty, charm, or personality. But this is not to be. However, Dr. Sloper is described by James as "a philosopher" - presumably of the Stoic variety, who says he expects nothing and thus will not be disappointed. He does not take out his frustration on his daughter - he is at least superficially too kindly and too just a man for this. But their relationship is already a curiously strained one. As for Mrs. Penniman, the Doctor has little respect for her qualities of mind.

Comment

It is already apparent that Doctor Sloper and his sister have differing images of Catherine. Neither, as James develops his portrait of Catherine's character, has much relevance to what she really is and what her needs are. This Section ends with the following description: "In reality, she was the softest creature in the world." The Doctor does not realize how much damage he is doing to her, how much she has already been damaged, by his attitude - nor, despite her air of sophisticated romanticism, does

Mrs. Penniman realize the damage which is being done by her preconceptions concerning Catherine.

SECTION III

At this point, the dramatic **exposition** is well advanced. We see Catherine now at sixteen. She gives the impression of excellent health, and physically this is so. She is rather inarticulate, but she does express herself in dress. Her "expectations," as was the term for her possible inheritance or financial standing, seemed considerable, for James (who often mentions specific incomes or sums of money, as in *The American*) uses this kind of reference in order to establish a certain kind of expectation of a character. The Doctor is very well-off, because an income of $20,000 per year, of which he saves half, is in terms of the financial values of the year 1835 a considerable fortune. As his only living child, Catherine of course stands to have a large inheritance. The Doctor, being the kind of man he is and having worked as hard as he has worked in his profession, will not wish to see this fortune squandered.

Dr. Sloper had moved his household, as he prospered, uptown in New York City-from the City Hall area, which socially had been the most desired area in the 1820s, to Washington Square, where in 1835 the ideal of "genteel retirement" was embodied, and right on the Square, around the corner from Fifth Avenue - the very originating point of this, one of the most famous Avenues of any major city in the world, Dr. Sloper purchased a most handsome house, as fitted his station in life. Mrs. Almond, the Doctor's younger sister, lived further uptown; she eventually had a family of nine children, and Catherine Sloper was often invited to the Almond home to fraternize with her cousins. As the children matured, the Almond boys went to college or directly into business careers. One of the daughters, at the time this Section ends was aged seventeen and engaged to marry a young stockbroker of about twenty. This fact leads directly into the central situation of the story: Catherine's meeting with Morris Townsend.

Comment

This Section establishes further atmosphere. The description of the Washington Square area in the second quarter of the nineteenth century is extremely well done; James's descriptions of cities often are able to get behind the facades, and this level of sheer description of one of the most famous areas of a great, if not the greatest, city accounts for the popularity of *Washington Square* among foreign readers of James. The other function of this section, besides those that contribute to the exposition and establishing atmosphere, is found in the explanation of how it is that Catherine Sloper comes to be introduced to the man who is to be her fiance, Morris Townsend.

SECTION IV

Marian Almond is Catherine's cousin, and as this Section opens Marian introduces to Catherine a young man named Morris Townsend, who is a cousin of Marian's future husband, Arthur Townsend. Catherine, who is often awkward socially especially where introductions are concerned, is immediately charmed by Morris Townsend, who appears quite handsome to her and begins to speak in such an easy manner to her that it is as if he had known her for years.

Morris is actually Arthur's second or third cousin. He had been "knocking about" for a number of years, and even as early as the first meeting between Catherine and Morris, James gives his readers the hint that Morris is somehow subtly defective, as though he had never taken root anywhere or established himself at anything. When he talks to Catherine, it is "the way a young man might talk in a novel; or, better still, in a play, on the stage...." This bit of characterization is, as we shall see, a very important one, for it introduces a basic Jamesian **theme**: what is "the real thing" (in the terms of the title of one of his short stories) as applied to human character? Morris acts a part, and we surmise this from the beginning. But what is he in reality?

Marian tells Catherine that she thinks Morris to be terribly conceited, but Catherine, in her inexperience, refuses to accept this evaluation. Meanwhile, Doctor Sloper, who is at the party, also addresses Catherine - he always speaks to her in a mildly ironic form, as he does here of her costume: "Is it possible that this magnificent person is my child?" he said. As they go home in their carriage, Catherine dissembles, for only the first or second time in her life. The Doctor already suspects that the young man had been paying attention to Catherine's rich, opulent clothing, which indicates an income of at least "eighty thousand a year." But when he asks her for the young man's name, she says that she doesn't know -and her father believes her.

Comment

James, subtly and with economy of words, by the end of Section IV has established the central situation which is to be acted out and resolved in this story. There is more than a hint that the Doctor believes the young man, whose name he does not even know, to have designs not only against his daughter but against her fortune. And there are legal facts stemming from the situation of the married woman in early nineteenth-century England and America (as well as other countries, of course), which make this issue more important to a man such as Dr. Sloper than it possibly would be now. A parent of a daughter, especially a parent with the social and financial standing of someone like Dr. Sloper, had to be rather careful, because once his daughter married, the legal control and even the title of her property would pass over to her husband, and there was then very little which could be done to help the lady if her husband chose to squander all of the money and property.

It is probable that one of the reasons James is so careful to establish Dr. Sloper's habits of thrift and industry is to provide motivation for the war he is to wage against the suit of Morris Townsend for the hand of his daughter. It is a matter of historical interest to note that the situation with respect to the status of the property of a married woman in England was not remedied until the passage by Parliament in 1882 of the Married Women's Property Act, which gave married women a certain measure of control over property which they brought with them to a marriage. The equivalent Act was established in the various states of the U.S. later - in any case, this would have been about a half-century after the action of *Washington Square*. A point to keep in mind is that James himself was well aware of the law governing the disposition of property; he had studied law for a year at Harvard Law School, as we have noted in the sketch of his career, and though he reacted against the view of human relations taken by the Common Law, he knew something of that law. This is another explanation for the fight which the Doctor is to put up against Morris Townsend. For if it took the Doctor most of his life to accumulate a comfortable amount of property, all of which might pass by inheritance to Catherine, the property could be squandered by an "adventurer" in a few days or weeks - and Dr. Sloper sees Morris as distinctly an adventurer.

SECTION V

Miss Sloper, as well as Morris Townsend, become more sharply-defined as characters at this point. They are thrown together at a meeting in the Doctor's home at Washington Square, which had really been arranged by Lavinia Penniman, who had mentioned to Morris that she would be pleased if he would call in company with his cousin Arthur. Therefore, on a Sunday afternoon, the two gentlemen appear. It is Arthur who speaks to Catherine, while Lavinia Penniman entertains Morris. They discuss the domestic arrangements which Arthur and Mrs. Almond's daughter are planning, including Arthur's theory that with New York City growing the way it is, one must move every three or four years to be in the most desirable section: right now, it is Washington Square, perhaps later it will be further uptown. Arthur jokes: the word Excelsior, meaning "still higher," or "ever upward," is not only the motto of New York State, it is also the title of a vaguely inspirational poem of that **theme**, by Longfellow, to which Arthur Townsend refers.

Arthur reveals that Morris Townsend has still not established himself in any business or profession. He has no family who can assist him, except one sister. One feels as this meeting proceeds that it is Mrs. Penniman, rather than Catherine, who is the more impelled to hope that Morris will take an interest in her. As the Section closes, Catherine is however becoming more interested in Morris.

Comment

The hint of a weakness in Morris Townsend's character and in his approach to life is further developed, and it already seems evident that Morris may be a charming man, but he is also an idler. Catherine is the kind of girl who may be taken in by such a person, because the defenses she should have-her knowledge of reality-have not been sufficiently developed. She is still an innocent, but in an unfortunate sense, and between Dr. Sloper and Lavinia Penniman, neither has given Catherine the kind of upbringing which would have properly equipped her. This kind of situation leads into another basic and most serious **theme** of Henry James: what happens when unschooled innocence is confronted by the darker side of life, by "the permanent ugly world into which all new worlds collapse," as R. P. Blackmur stated in his "Preface" to *The Golden Bowl*? This is a problem which faces the heroine of what is possibly James's greatest novel, *The Golden Bowl*; it faces Isabel Archer, in *The Portrait of a Lady*, and in a different way, Christopher Newman in *The American*. Here, at a more modest but more understandable level, the same problem or question confronts Catherine Sloper. It is hard to describe Morris Townsend as evil, in the sense that certain of the characters, say in *The Turn of the Screw*, *The Jolly Corner*, or *The Wings of the Dove* are or become evil. It may be that Morris's character is merely shabby, not evil. And at this point the further question may be raised: is the Doctor guiltless?

SECTION VI

As this part of the novel begins, Mrs. Penniman tells Dr. Sloper, who has returned home just after the departure of the young men, that Morris Townsend has been there visiting, at the Doctor's own residence in Washington Square. The Doctor hasn't even known Morris by name previous to this event, and he tells Lavinia Penniman that the next time Morris calls he, Austin Sloper, would like to meet him, so that they had better call him. Five days later, Morris comes, but Dr. Sloper is not at home. So Catherine sees Morris alone, with Mrs. Penniman as chaperone.

Mrs. Penniman evaluates Morris as a young man who has great force of character, with a keen, resolute, brilliant nature. In this she couldn't be more mistaken, but at this point is yet to find it out. Her romantic fantasy about Morris has not yet been subjected to the serious attention of Dr. Sloper. Thus, she leaves Morris and Catherine to talk for about an hour. Dr. Sloper returns just after Morris leaves, and Catherine feels impelled to tell him that Morris had been there. "Well, my dear, did he propose to you today?" are the Doctor's words, spoken mostly in jest, because, for one thing, he cannot believe that anyone would be interested in Catherine for herself, though he realizes already that they might be interested in her for her inheritance. Catherine's answer, "Perhaps he will propose the next time," is not quite what he expects, and Catherine goes upstairs, leaving the Doctor to ponder her words.

Dr. Sloper now begins to inform himself seriously about the character of Morris Townsend. He learns, from discussions with Mrs. Almond, that Morris Townsend is really of a rather distant branch of the family, that Morris has a sister named Mrs. Montgomery, who is a widow with a bit of property and five children to bring up. She lives on Second Avenue, also in New York, and the Doctor determines to call on her soon, for he has heard that Mrs. Montgomery thinks of her brother as having talents by which he might perhaps distinguish himself, but so far he has done nothing with them. Morris has been in the Navy when very young, has traveled all over the world, and is now over thirty. Having been both a wanderer and now an adventurer, in the sense of "fortune-hunter," it may be he has come back to America hoping to start life seriously. But how?

Elizabeth Almond calls her brother's attention, in case he has forgotten, to the fact that Catherine has the prospect of $30,000 a year of income-a very huge sum then - and that this will make her most attractive to suitors, who may be the wrong kind. This puts an idea into his head: Catherine has never impressed her father as unattractive; he just cannot think that anyone will be interested in her. He does not come to any conclusion, except that he decides to find out more about Morris, to begin with, from his sister, Mrs. Montgomery. As he leaves, he recalls the latter's address.

Comment

Under the placidity of this upper-middle-class society life, as it may be described, there is distinct action here, stemming from the conflict of motives in the characters involved. What the Doctor is about may seem to present-day readers as cruel prying tainted with needless suspicion. But he is a man of the world, and he has justifiable doubts about the young man Morris's motives. One must consider Dr. Sloper's position: his financial position, and beyond and above that, his ethical position. Is what he is doing praiseworthy? He would think so, and would probably tell himself, if he were aware, that he is acting from the purest motives. But is he? James's own position, though it is free of overt moralizing, will become quite clear as the story develops.

WASHINGTON SQUARE

SECTION VII

At the beginning of this Section, Dr. Sloper is not really seriously troubled by the situation, and is honestly willing to give the young man the benefit of every doubt. Catherine, after all, is twenty-two, and there is a danger of her remaining unmarried. He wonders, however, whether Catherine can possibly be loved for her moral worth, or only for her fortune. And the fact that Morris is poor is not necessarily a discouragement-Catherine will have enough of an inheritance for two, if only her husband turns out to be prudent and of sound character, unlikely to prey upon her for her fortune.

To get to know Morris better, Dr. Sloper invites him to dinner. He perceives that Morris does have ability, as he speaks to him over the excellent table wine. "I don't think I like him," the Doctor concludes. Morris is very quick to sense this, as he says to Catherine afterwards. Morris tells Mrs. Penniman this later also. "He thinks I am all wrong." These perceptions do exist on both sides, though they all well-hidden. The Doctor's conclusion about Morris Townsend is that he is not a gentleman-he's insinuating, clever, plausible, and familiar, but has an essentially vulgar nature, in Dr. Sloper's eyes. Mrs. Almond suggests that perhaps the Doctor is too hasty in forming judgments about people. But he is convinced, in large part from his professional experience which involves ability to make close observations of the character as well as the human body, that he is right. As Mrs. Almond adds, the Doctor may very well be right about Morris Townsend, but the thing is to make Catherine see what he does.

Comment

The enmity and ill-will between Morris and Dr. Sloper is now perceptible, though the two men haven't spoken a word to each other about this. It is more a feeling, a perception, but it is to have a great effect on both of their lives from this point on. This is the Jamesian equivalent of-to be quite crude - the Gunfight at the O.K. Corral. The violence, the combat of life occurs; it will occur in James's stories, but what actions are seen must stand for what is not seen. The falling-out of Morris and the Doctor occurs over a bottle of wine at dinner, with no word spoken - and the question which James seems to have been asking, though he didn't phrase it this way, is this: Are the men reacting to each other's true characters, or is it a pre-conceived image they have of each other?

SECTION VIII

The break between Dr. Sloper and Morris (not that they have known each other that long) still has not come into the open.

Their relationship is still civil, and Morris calls at the Sloper residence regularly, and as Dr. Sloper more than suspects, Morris has "plenty of leisure on his hands." He is not engaged in a gainful occupation. Catherine has an imagined idea of what it is to be in love, but she has no sense of her "rights," because her upbringing has been too stifling. She is too grateful for the interest Morris shows in her to be capable of having an ideal sort of relationship with him.

Catherine has not discussed Morris with her father any further, and has not even mentioned to him that Morris is calling at the house. The Doctor realizes that something like this is going on, but since he is a just man, it does not even occur to him to ask the servants for details. He is determined to give his daughter her liberty, and to interfere only if he sees a proven danger to her. So far, he suspects the danger-Morris's fortune-hunting-but has no proof. The person he finally approaches is Mrs. Penniman, and he asks her what is going on in the house. Why hasn't she let him know, he inquires, that Morris has been visiting the house three or four times a week in his absence? Her answer is that she respects confidences. Morris has, further, given her certain confidential information about himself and his prospects which she will not violate. He is, in her eyes, an attractive young man who has experienced many misfortunes. The Doctor indicates to her that he is going to ask Morris not to call-to "leave Catherine alone." He is incensed at his sister, because he feels that she has been encouraging Morris in what is obviously a suit for the hand of Catherine, in defiance of Dr. Sloper's wishes. Morris is "wild," or so he has told Mrs. Penniman, and he has few friends, no money, and no profession. But he is looking for a position, while apparently existing on the support furnished by his widowed sister, hardly an admirable arrangement on his part. As the Section ends, it is clear that Dr. Sloper is convinced that Morris is looking for a position: "here, over there in the front parlor. The position of husband of a weak-minded woman with a large fortune would suit him to perfection." But Mrs. Penniman objects to the last characterization-she does not believe, she tells her brother, that Catherine is at all weak-minded. And though she has been wrong about many things, it seems that she is more correct about this one issue than her brother. Catherine can manage her own affairs, she thinks, and she should be allowed to.

Comment

With the end of this Section, the battle has been established, and one may say that the expository material has been completed. There is just enough of this material to let the reader know what the issues are. As discussed briefly in the following chapter, the first eight Sections form a major unit in the structure of *Washington Square*.

SECTIONS I-VIII

In the first eight Sections of *Washington Square*, the **exposition** is concluded and the principals are introduced and developed. Much more is suggested than is overtly stated, and James brilliantly and convincingly builds up an atmosphere which is an organic part of the story - the reader should keep in mind the title: it is not "Jealousy," nor is it "Family Intrigue" nor "The Eternal Triangle," nor "Greed," nor "Fathers and Daughters," nor "Fathers and Lovers," although all of these rather hackneyed titles could be made to fit. It is *Washington Square*, and as James chose his words, and especially his names and titles very carefully, this is of significance, for the City itself is a form of actor in the drama which is being played out in this novel.

There is a certain very narrow social stratum and even geographic area of life in a great city, at a very definite period of time. But what part does the City play? This is a question which must be answered as the action unfolds further.

The fictional technique in the first eight Sections shows precision, economy, and restraint. Of the three, the precision of statement may be the most outstanding feature of the writing. The fictional technique in the sheer telling of the story - the authority which presents the story to the reader - is that known as the Omniscient Narrator. In other stories of Henry James - take the much later *The Beast in the Jungle* (1903), which is among the most famous, as an example - James used other, more sophisticated and developed techniques. In the latter story, he uses what is called the method of the "Central Intelligence." This means that we see through the eyes of only one character, in *The Beast in the Jungle* the man John Marcher, about whom the story revolves. Here, too, the basic **theme** of Jamesian vampirism is illustrated, though James shows it at one degree more of subtlety, in that John Marcher, the herovictim of *The Beast in the Jungle*, is victimized and made to suffer not by a person, but by an idea which he cannot get out of his head: that something illustrious, the "beast," is to happen to him at some point in his life. Thus, he condemns the lady, May Bartram, to death because he withholds from her that which she needs to keep her alive, which is love. It is only at her grave that he realizes that the beast has already sprung: that which had happened to him was that "no passion had ever touched him." The method by which the story is told is called the method of the Central Intelligence - there is one character, a single mind, who filters and evaluates all of the action while being itself placed in the dramatic situation. Such is John Marcher; we see reality through his eyes. But, after all, it is his story.

In *Washington Square*, which of course belongs to an earlier stage in James's artistic development - two decades earlier, in fact - a simpler method is used, dictated in large part by the fact that the three central characters all have extreme importance, though if we were forced to choose we would probably have to say that the story is primarily Catherine Sloper's. The simpler method of telling a story is that of the Omniscient Narrator - he knows, whoever he is, what goes on in the consciousness of each of the characters. This is not the same method as that of the so-called stream-of-consciousness narrative, as practiced perhaps most successfully by James Joyce in *Ulysses* or William Faulkner in *The Sound and the Fury*, among recent writers in English. This is a psychological technique which attempts to reveal the subconscious as well as the conscious mind. James does not do this. What he does have is a consciousness, which we can call Omniscient because it has a vantage-point from which it can see and describe the actions of all of the characters in the story. The Omniscient Narrative method is more historical, less psychological, and less dependent upon the area of the unconscious or subconscious mind than is the method of the Central Intelligence - but the Omniscient Narrative is necessary when there are several very important characters in a story who interact, and this is assuredly the case in *Washington Square*.

We, and James, are in the position of an audience watching a drama as we read the first eight sections of *Washington Square*. What we can see is mainly scenery and external actions - and in fact *Washington Square* has been dramatized. We make certain inferences from the actions we observe; they are not made for us completely, nor should they be - and this is what is meant by the dramatic method of **exposition** in the first eight Sections of this novel.

SECTION IX

Dr. Sloper and his family go to Mrs. Almond's residence on Sunday night for a general gathering, as is their custom. On the Sunday some five days after the conversation just preceding, the Doctor is in the sitting-room of his sister, from which he withdraws for a few minutes to discuss some point of business with his brother-in-law, Mrs. Almond's husband. When he returns, he sees Morris, seated on a small sofa next to Catherine. Almost-almost but not quite, does Dr. Sloper pity his daughter, for her plainness (as he sees it). He turns away so that Catherine will be spared the indignity of believing that he is watching her. "She thinks me a cruel tyrant," he observes to himself - and he is too intelligent to wish to reinforce this thought in her mind. His view of the situation, though, is still that she is a plain, unattractive young girl who is dazzled by having an outwardly charming and pleasing young man pay attention to her.

Nevertheless, the Doctor wishes to learn more about Morris. Perhaps he has misjudged him. He crosses over to where Morris is standing near the fireplace, and says: "I am told you are looking out for a position." Dr. Sloper adds that he believes that Morris is intelligent and talented, but Morris indicates that in terms of training he is fit for very little in the way of position. The Doctor continues to praise his intelligence. "You advise me, then, not to despair?" So Morris says, as he looks directly at the Doctor, who determines that this statement has, perhaps, a double meaning. Is Morris talking about a professional situation, or is he talking about the possibility that he may be given the Doctor's permission to marry Catherine? In terms of the revelation of his character even we, the readers, are not sure just what Morris means. But we have a further idea when he asks the Doctor if he has something to suggest.

Controlling his chagrin at what he considers Morris's impudence, Dr. Sloper says that he sometimes hears of jobs - invariably outside New York. Morris says he can't consider this - he serves as the tutor to the children of his widowed sister. This scene is of course on two levels - the open meanings of what the two men say to one another, and the hidden meaning: "Why don't you decide to leave town?" implies Dr. Sloper. The Doctor further decides that he must see Mrs. Montgomery, Morris's sister, and Mrs. Almond says that she will arrange it.

Meanwhile, Morris has now told what amounts to a lie to Catherine: he tells her that her father has insulted him, so that he cannot visit Washington Square again to see her. "He has taunted me with my poverty," says Morris. This is untrue. He is playing on the sympathies of Catherine, when he asks her if she will meet him secretly elsewhere, perhaps in the park at Washington Square, but not in the house. Catherine says that she is not brave, and asks that if they meet, it be in her house rather than elsewhere. Morris is a bit surprised at this, but he has scored several points in the contest, so he is not alarmed.

Comment

It is now, not before the events of the ninth Section, that we know something really definitive about the character of Morris Townsend. From all evidences, Dr. Sloper has been quite accurate in his judgment of the young man. But will Dr. Sloper's actions be the right ones, to protect his daughter from Morris's designs? The matter is left by James very much up in the air.

SECTION X

The next day-for Morris will not wait in following up the advantage he thinks he has gained-Catherine speaks with him. Morris proposes marriage; Catherine determines that she will speak to her father that night, and Morris must speak to him the following day.

Morris, as clever as he is in such affairs, which hints at previous experience, suggests to Catherine that her father will say of him that he is "mercenary." He uses all the tricks of rhetoric to get her to believe that he is not after her money, though she professes to believe that such a thought had never occurred to her. Catherine is, as Morris reminds her, "of age." She can legally marry without her father's consent. But what of the fortune which she may or may not bring to her future husband? Her father controls the purse strings, and she herself suspects already that her father will never give his consent to the marriage. Turning on Morris, she asks once again for his assurance that he loves her. Is he quite sure? she asks. This may be the forerunner of doubts which she is harboring about Morris-or perhaps she is just being honest with herself, as well as with him.

Comment

Catherine is actually proving herself so far to be more level-headed and sensible than either of the men in the story, and certainly more realistic than her impossibly romantic aunt, Mrs. Penniman. The question is whether her strength will be equal to the combat in which she is now engaged.

SECTION XI

That evening, Catherine says to her father that she is engaged to be married, and that the young man is Mr. Morris Townsend. And it is "serious." Dr. Sloper's dry comment is that perhaps Mr. Townsend ought to have come first to speak to him. Catherine says that she had been hesitant about asking her father first, because she was afraid her father didn't like Morris. Dr. Sloper indeed agrees with this: he doesn't like Mr. Townsend; he doesn't know that much about him, but then, neither does Catherine.

At this point, after further fencing, the Doctor is prevailed upon to give his reasons for his opinion. Catherine has already been warned about the statement which would be made: that Morris was "mercenary." The Doctor gives all of the usual arguments, arranged in the most logical and succinct fashion: Morris has led a life of dissipation, he has spent a fortune on pleasure, he has no profession, and he would be very likely to waste Catherine's fortune as well as his own. Catherine defends Morris, and says that such money as he had inherited was a very small amount which wouldn't have lasted long. As the interview ends, Dr. Sloper says that he will see Morris on the following day.

Comment

The Doctor's dryly ironic attitude toward Catherine's telling him of her engagement indicates that his mind is still made up - and what we know of him makes it rather clear that he is not likely to change his mind. Still, there is hope that his affection for Catherine will lead him to reconsider and give his consent to the suit of Morris Townsend.

One interesting aspect of the story so far is what it leaves out. We know that the Doctor is still maintaining a large, fashionable, and lucrative medical practice; that he must, by the nature and demands of his profession, be available at all times, for crises made more acute by the really backward state of medicine in the early part of the nineteenth century. But none of this drama shows through the sedate description of the surface of life at Washington Square in the 1830s and 40s. In this lack of attention to the ways in which his characters actually earn their livings - the major concern for most people, then as now - James has been attacked as one not in contact with everyday reality, a snob, a turncoat who sneered at his "practical" country, and a number of other uncomplimentary things besides. We have no time to refute these charges, here, except to say that James had other concerns than the "everyday-making-a-living" one, and that these concerns can be proven to be valid. The proof is in the works of fiction themselves.

SECTION XII

In this Section occurs the long interview between Morris Townsend and his most unwilling prospective father-in-law, Dr. Sloper. Morris calls on Dr. Sloper at his home in Washington Square. While the level of the conversation seems rather elegant, even pompous, it is a deadly serious game that the two men are playing. Morris has recognized that the Doctor doesn't like him, and professes to attribute this to his, Morris's, being poor. The Doctor denies this; the young man's lack of means is not the primary objection, but his lack of a profession and of prospects therein is a concern.

Morris says that he can offer the word of a gentleman that he guarantees a life-time of devotion to Catherine, but the Doctor retorts that while the sentiments are fine, such guarantees can have little value, the world being what it is. Dr. Sloper adds that he likes Morris in most ways, but not as a son-in-law. "In any other capacity, I am perfectly prepared to like you. As a son-in-law, I abominate you," he says. Morris outlines his financial situation; he says that he is living on a little money which is left from his inheritance. Then the conversation becomes more heated; Morris will not give up Catherine, and neither will the Doctor budge an inch from his position that he will not permit the marriage; that his daughter is dutiful and will respect his wishes. As the scene ends, Morris assures the Doctor that Catherine has pledged herself to him, and he will not retreat from his rights.

Comment

The urbanity of the conversation between Morris Townsend and Dr. Sloper masks its violence and aggressiveness. Morris seems stubborn about his right to be chosen by Catherine; the Doctor is equally as set in his belief that Morris is not the right man to be his son-in-law.

On the surface, the situation seems clear and conventional enough, and must have happened millions of times in "real life." What is important here is what is left out: Catherine's welfare - any consideration of her wishes and of the validity of these wishes. After all, it is her life. Even if Morris Townsend is not the right husband for her, she should have the right to choose, and the right not to be tampered with by being treated as an object, not a person. Yet Catherine is not a consideration in this scene, and the whole thing is a chilling spectacle because of the neglect of Catherine's interests.

Of the two men, the Doctor seems to be regarded here and elsewhere by James as the worse. We can surmise this in the light of James's views on conduct-see the earlier essay on James's morality. Morris does not convince us one way or the other at this point; he may be sincere in his protestations of love for Catherine, and may not be scheming to get her inheritance. But the Doctor has already demonstrated his inflexibility.

SECTION XIII

This brief Section consists of a meeting between Dr. Sloper, and his married sister, Mrs. Almond; the purpose of the interview, of course, is further discussion of Morris Townsend and his proposed marriage to Catherine. Because this Section is so short, it can easily be overlooked-but it contains a key insight into Dr. Sloper's character. Dr. Sloper simply says that he will consult Mrs. Montgomery, Morris's sister, and find out more about Morris. Mrs. Almond cautions him that obviously Morris's sister can hardly be expected to talk objectively about Morris, especially "when it's a question of thirty thousand a year coming into a family."

The Doctor is too positive about his ability to read character. He "had passed his life in estimating people," because of course a physician must always do this-it sometimes being as important for a doctor to know what kind of patient he has as for him to know what kind of illness the patient has. This is part of Dr. Sloper's basic character or personality defect, which he has little or no insight into. The Doctor further perceives the difficulties with his other sister, Lavinia; she is on the "side" of Morris in this contest, and he is clever enough to see that when Lavinia favors a cause, it is damaged by her help, because she is not really able to benefit the causes on whose side she enlists, having relatively little common sense.

Comment

The point of this **episode** is the extent of the Doctor's self-deception. He is simply not able to see that the situation is other than he imagines it. Of Catherine and Lavinia Penniman, he says: "They are both afraid of me, harmless as I am ... And it is on that that I build-on the salutary terror I inspire."

But one should not base his conduct on terrorism. Even though the location of the story is the genteel Washington Square of the earlier nineteenth century, under the surface there is the kind of primitive combat practiced as well in pre-historic times as today: several people wanting things which are, or seem to be, mutually exclusive so that there must be a winner and a loser. And the Doctor, with his inflexible will and his vast pride, has determined that he will not be the loser.

It should be noted that up to this point, we are more sure of the Doctor's outlook than we are of that of Morris or of Catherine. Catherine may not be as silly and dull, nor Morris so venal and irresponsible, as the Doctor supposes. But of Dr. Sloper himself, we have already seen, by his actions, what manner of man he is.

SECTIONS IX-XIII

These five Sections, like the eight preceding them, form a natural unit. It may be said that Sections IX-XIII concentrate less on **exposition**, and more on character and plot development. It is rather clear that by the end of this second unit, the enmity between Morris Townsend and Dr. Sloper has come into the open, and that Catherine is beginning to be torn in her affections between the two men-further, that Catherine is less the deceiver than the deceived.

Of the three really primary characters, we seem to have attained a knowledge of the Doctor's make-up first. He is presented as a more and more selfish and ruthless character. In the light of the remarks made earlier about Henry James's moral vision, it can be seen that Dr. Sloper is also becoming increasingly guilty of psychological aggressiveness and moral vampirism. The Doctor belongs, then, in the company of such Jamesian vampires as Gilbert Osmond, of *The Portrait of a Lady*, the Bellegardes, in *The American*, and perhaps the Narrator [never named] of *The Sacred Fount*. Dr. Sloper is a simpler version of these three, or perhaps it is just that the story, relying as the title implies more on the atmosphere of specific surroundings at a definite time and place in Washington Square than do the other works mentioned, is outwardly simpler. But actually the ramifications of the Doctor's conduct are quite complex, for they involve his attempt to deny freedom to another human being, Catherine, in a manner which simply must not be allowed, according to the basic moral view of Henry James. And it is this denial of a basic freedom, which in turn robs one of life itself, or of that which can make life worth living, of which the Doctor stands accused by his own self-revealed character, by the end of this second major unit of *Washington Square*.

SECTION XIV

Dr. Sloper calls on Morris's sister, Mrs. Montgomery, and finds her an agreeable woman. Unfortunately, he brings his preconceptions about Morris with him, and while they have a very frank conversation in her modest house on Second Avenue, the Doctor is more convinced than ever of the basic weakness of Morris's character. "What sort of gentleman is your brother?" asks the Doctor. Mrs. Montgomery replies that it is hard to answer such a question. The Doctor persists. He says that if Catherine were to marry without his permission, she would have not a penny from him, though she would have still ten thousand dollars a year from her mother's estate. Mrs. Montgomery has an interesting answer to this: "That is too much money to get possession of by marrying. I don't think it would be right."

Mrs. Montgomery sees that the Doctor does not like Morris, and asks him why this is the case. "He strikes me as selfish and shallow," is the answer. The Doctor sees that everything else about Morris may be admirable; he has no evidence. But Morris is still not the kind of man to whom he wishes to entrust his only child, Catherine, as a wife. Dr. Sloper "divides people into classes," as he tells Mrs. Montgomery, and he is never or seldom mistaken. He says that Morris is the kind who is the ruination of women, and because of his attractive physical appearance can get women to do practically anything for him. The Doctor also guesses shrewdly that Mrs. Montgomery has "suffered greatly" on account of her brother, and further, that she has been giving him money. Dr. Sloper offers to help out the woman, as he knows that she has five children and is poor-but she has her pride, and it is a proper pride, in contrast to that of the Doctor. As the scene ends, Mrs. Montgomery refuses to say anything in criticism of her brother. Instead, she says that she would like to know Catherine, and suddenly gives the Doctor this advice, which is what he wants to hear: "Don't let her marry him!"

Comment

It is in the last lines of this Section that a puzzle arises. Dr. Sloper assumes that Mrs. Montgomery does not condone the possible marriage - "Don't let her marry him!" - because of the weakness of Morris's character. Actually, all of the implications are that Mrs. Montgomery is, despite her ill-fortune and her poverty, a most honest and remarkable woman, who tells the Doctor this for the sake of Morris and Catherine, as well as for her own sake. For she perceives that the Doctor would, money or not, be an impossible, dangerous, and even sinister person to have for a father-in-law for Morris. She sees that Dr. Sloper makes up his mind too quickly; that he has a destructive pride of will. She rejects him as a member of the family; she is too polite to say this in so many words, but that is the motivating force behind her final statement, which is hard to explain otherwise.

WASHINGTON SQUARE

. . . .

SECTION XV

Catherine, meanwhile, behaves rather strangely, from Dr. Sloper's point of view. "She will do as I have bidden her" says the Doctor. Catherine has meanwhile not seen Morris; she has written him a long letter, of five pages. The import of it is that she wishes he will not visit her at home until she has thought further about the situation. Morris replies with violent protestations of love, and a wish to rescue her from her "cruel slavery."

Catherine again replies, more briefly, that she is in great torment of mind and must think further. It seems that Morris does not give her quite the same account of his interview with Dr. Sloper as James gives, but we know that he has a tendency to exaggerate to his own advantage. Mrs. Penniman, meanwhile, her romantic imagination aroused, arranges a secret meeting with Morris to report on developments, and she meets him at an oyster saloon, or rather cheap restaurant, on Seventh Avenue.

Morris arrives half an hour late, and exerts self-control, as James tells us, in order that he will not spoil his "image" before Mrs. Penniman. But he thinks her a meddlesome old fool.

Comment

This Section provides more insight into the character of Morris Townsend. He is not the very straightest kind of person; James himself tells us this, with the information about his double-dealing (1) in his letter to Catherine, and (2) in his meeting with Mrs. Penniman.

However, this is not the same thing as saying that Dr. Sloper has been doing the right thing in his treatment of either Morris or Catherine. The Doctor does not seem to realize just what harm he is doing to his daughter. If she wishes to make a mistake, after reflecting on it for a considerable time, the implication is beginning to dawn here, in the light of James's moral vision, that she should be allowed to make the mistake; that neither her father nor anyone else can really give her valid advice.

SECTION XVI

In his interview with Mrs. Penninman, Morris is hard. Mrs. Penniman, romantically, counsels Morris that the only thing which will bring the Doctor to approve of the match will be a fait accompli-if the marriage has already taken place. Thus, she tells him to elope with Catherine. "The woman's an idiot," thinks Morris of Mrs. Penniman. But he plays out his part. She tells him that such an elopement will tend to prove to the Doctor that Morris is not simply interested in Catherine's money, because he will not receive much if he goes against the Doctor's wishes. But Morris says that in part he is interested in the money. Morris asks about Dr. Sloper's will, and listens to Mrs. Penniman's further account of why he should consider eloping with Catherine. He escorts her home to Washington Square, and as he contemplates the house of the Slopers, concludes what a comfortable house it must be.

Comment

This scene illustrates the mixed motives at work in Morris's mind, as in those of all men and women. Morris is a complex being whom the Doctor insists on reducing to a simplistic level. Morris is interested in the money and the house. He is, as he says to Mrs. Penniman, sincerely grateful for Catherine's love of him. Morris is, in other words, a mixture of good and evil motives, and he seems quite intelligent in that he admits these frankly to himself. The Doctor likewise has a mixture of motives, but he is not as frank with himself; he is too self-righteous. Therefore, it is the Doctor who has the greater fault. Mrs. Penniman is admittedly a shallow and silly woman, but her motivations are understandable; she wishes to live vicariously in the romance of Catherine and Morris, since she has had so little romance in her own rather tragic life.

SECTION XVII

Mrs. Penniman, the busy body, now gives an account of the preceding interview with Morris to Catherine. She tells Catherine that Morris had said he is ready to marry her any day, in spite of her father's opposition. He is very miserable, she adds. He is afraid of only one thing: that she, Catherine, "will be afraid of her father." To which Catherine adds: "I am afraid of my father." Mrs. Penniman reproaches her for not being brave in going to the defense of her lover. She answers that she has promised her father. She "fears" him almost in a Biblical sense; that she pays attention to his words, in the same sense, perhaps, as St. Paul stated as a motto: "Fear God; Honor the king." By this he meant that people should have respect for both Divine and secular authority, and amongst the latter kinds of authority, ultimately derivable from religious sanctions and principles, would be respect for the authority of parents over their children. But this is simply implied, and indeed James may not have meant it. It turns out, at the end of this Section, that Catherine and her aunt have a falling-out, however delicately it is disguised. Catherine no longer trusts Mrs. Penniman, and is resentful that she, any more than her father, should try to force her to do certain things against her will, whether to marry or not to marry Morris.

Comment

Here the vampiristic web surrounding Catherine is made more intense and strangling; she is under conflicting pressures, and something will have to happen. Will she be strong enough to do what is best for all concerned? Further, as James asks the question, why should she be subjected to this kind of baleful influence at all? Right or wrong, it is Catherine herself who must take responsibility for her own destiny; she must choose, and neither her father, nor Morris, nor Mrs. Penniman have the right to interfere with her choice.

SECTION XVIII

Catherine meditates further about her problems here. Finally, she tells her father that she desires to see Morris again. "To bid him good-bye?" her father asks. No, that is not the reason, because he is not going away. She tells the Doctor that she has asked Morris to wait. One of the crucial points in this scene occurs when Dr. Sloper tells Catherine: "It is better to be unhappy for three months and get over it, than for many years and never get over it."

This is exactly the point: the Doctor is wrong here. He still judges Morris as a "selfish idler." But he has elevated his own prejudices to the level and status of revealed truth, and he cannot stand to have Catherine or anyone else refute these prejudices. The ending of this Section is terrible in its intensity, for the Doctor, while he "was sorry for her ... was so sure he was right." "By Jove," he said to himself, "I believe she will stick!" What he means by this is that she will stand by Morris, though not necessarily marry him. He sees that the situation has its comical side; "comical" is the exact word James uses, and this is crux of the Doctor's almost unforgivable offense.

Comment

Here the Doctor shows his intense selfishness, which is even worse than that of Morris Townsend. The Doctor plays upon the sympathies of Catherine, but he finds her problems humorous, or "comical." In the light of the moral picture presented in the Jamesian world, as stated previously, the Doctor's offense against Life and Freedom is the worst possible one within the terms of the story of *Washington Square*.

SECTION XIX

The Doctor informs Mrs. Penniman that "high-treason" is a capital offense. What he means by this is that he expects Mrs. Penniman to keep away from further meddling in the case. He is a distinguished physician, he reminds Mrs. Penniman, and therefore he knows what is best for Catherine, and that she will not die of disappointment in love. On the other hand, Mrs. Penniman reminds him, tartly, that his distinction in medicine had not prevented him from losing two members of his own family: his wife and his son. She is impressed by her own daring in going so far, and he threatens her indirectly by saying that he may be losing the company of a third: Mrs. Penniman. By that he suggests that he will throw Mrs. Penniman out, poverty or not, if she persists. He tells her that she lacks common sense, and in this he is perfectly right, as we have seen.

But the Doctor lacks uncommon sense. He tells Mrs. Penniman how to conduct herself if she wishes to remain living in his house. And this may be his right, but he has not the sense to see that in his treatment of his daughter he is merely killing her, at least killing her spirit. As the scene ends, Mrs. Penniman is consoling Catherine, who takes a surprisingly matter-of-fact attitude, and Catherine still tells herself that she must be an undutiful daughter to behave thus to her father.

Comment

The purpose of this Section is to build up the tension and the suspense further. Catherine seems to be placed in an impossible situation, and it is miraculous that she has been able thus far to survive so well.

SECTION XX

In this crucial Section, Morris Townsend comes to call at Washington Square. Her father is out. She tells Morris, who has said that she should have "decided sooner," that she had no thoughts of giving him up. But her father is unmoved. Morris suddenly asks her if she will marry him immediately, and she asks him whether it is not better to wait. Morris plays on her sympathies, accusing her of not being sincere. "Marry me next week," he says to her. She is smart enough to guess, even without his telling her, that Mrs. Penniman has put this idea into Morris's head.

They discuss money. She hears the deadly word, "disinherited," but it is not clear why the idea is so dreadful to her, because, after all, she will have enough money from her mother's estate. As the scene ends, Morris asks her again to marry him, and she says that she will do so as soon as he pleases.

Comment

Here there seems to be an understanding between Morris and Catherine. Actually, they are drifting farther apart. Morris seems not only puzzled by Catherine's sudden consent to marry him when he wishes; he also seems taken aback by it. Catherine's heart is described as "childlike" by James, but more in the sense of her innocence than of her naivete or lack of good sense. For of the four principals, if one counts Mrs. Penniman as a principal, Catherine really has the most common sense, although she is given credit for the least by the others.

SECTIONS XIV-XX

By the end of this, the third unit of the story-if one persists in regarding *Washington Square* as a kind of domestic five-act tragedy (and we have not yet established whether the story is of really tragic import), we see further interactions among the principal characters, and gradually Catherine seems to be emerging as the most sensible and the most admirable character, though she is discounted as such by her inflexible father, her foolish and overly-romantic aunt, and her weak and vacillating lover.

This third unit proceeds by rather straight dialogue and narration. The focus has shifted somewhat from the general picture of an environment, Washington Square, to the particular web of relationships among the central characters, who are increasingly vampiristic.

One must keep in mind what is involved here; nothing less than the lifelong happiness and well-being of four people. Even for Mrs. Penniman, the stakes are becoming too high; her security is involved, because if her brother chooses, he can exclude her from his house, and she has little or no means of support. Morris might be rescued by this marriage. His sister really seems to have confidence in him, and has much less confidence in the Doctor's suitability as a prospective in-law. But it is Catherine who is of absolutely primary interest here. She will not be able to please everyone by her conduct, but she has done as well as possible under the circumstances.

Catherine is being maneuvered into a situation from which there seems no escape. Each of the other three characters wants her to behave in a certain way, to please him (her) - but these ways of behavior are mutually exclusive. If she marries Morris after a long wait, she displeases him - or does she? – and her aunt, who entertains rather madly romantic notions of elopement and flight. While her father will never forgive her if she marries Morris under any circumstances at all. If, on the other hand, she gives up Morris, she gives up what she really wants, which is to be his wife-a choice freely made on her part, rightly or wrongly, and she pleases her father, which she wants to do as far as possible. How, then, will she resolve this situation?

SECTION XXI

By observing that Catherine is "going to stick," Dr. Sloper means of course that she will go through with her engagement; he is not absolutely sure that she will marry Morris. The tone and tenor of the observation at the end of Section XX on the part of the Doctor shows pretty clearly that he is experimenting with human life, much as Dr. Rappacini did with his daughter, in the famous story by Nathaniel Hawthorne, "Rappacini's Daughter." Mrs. Penniman accuses Dr. Sloper of being "shockingly cold-blooded" and he rather delights in this description. He has determined to take Catherine to Europe to polish her up a little bit and to enable her to forget Morris Townsend.

Mrs. Penniman loses no time in arranging a meeting with Morris in which she communicates to him the plans of the Doctor. She plays on his sympathies, telling Morris that she may herself be in the streets soon because the Doctor has had a falling out with her. But just then Morris tells her that as soon as he wishes, Catherine will consent to a private marriage. And then, most curiously, Mrs. Penniman puts another thought into his head - that Catherine loves him so much that he "may do anything." This seems to include a postponement of the marriage. The declaration is an ambiguous one. Morris himself is not quite sure what it means.

Comment

Why does Mrs. Penniman put another doubt into Morris's mind, just when he seems on the point of being resolved to marry Catherine? There are several possibilities: the older woman has finally acknowledged her jealousy of Catherine. Or, more practically, she believes her brother quite capable of turning her out of his house, as he will blame her for the marriage. In any case, she is still meddling with Catherine's life, in her officious and shallow way. It is rather certain that James means to suggest exactly this in his portrayal of Mrs. Penniman at this point.

SECTION XXII

Actually, Morris had exaggerated somewhat in suggesting that Catherine had agreed to marry him. Morris had not set a day; he is still afraid that his prospects of inheriting, with Catherine, a fortune, will be dimmed or defeated entirely if he goes through too early with the marriage. He must work out Dr. Sloper as the "unknown quantity." Meanwhile Dr. Sloper, having thought out a plan, is giving his daughter the "silent treatment." He barely speaks to her. Meanwhile, she tells him that she has been seeing Mr. Townsend again, even while she feels guilty about doing so because it transgresses her father's wishes. She says that they will probably marry "fairly soon." This means, she adds, perhaps four or five months. He says, why not put it off for six months and go on a European tour with him. She says he is too good; she oughtn't to accept his generosity if she plans to go against him in the matter of the marriage. But the Doctor, deciding to keep to himself his worry at that particular idea expressed by his daughter, perseveres. "If I live with you, I ought to obey you," says Catherine to her father, and upon discerning that this is her own idea, and not second-hand, he is unaccountably worried. But the European plan stands.

Comment

The prospective marriage has been put off and put off, until now the psychological moment seems to have gone. Catherine would like a European trip, but her main reason for going on it is a sense of duty toward her father. Morris has not been really insistent about the marriage, and therefore, neither has Catherine. The Doctor's view is that such a trip will help Catherine to forget the young man.

Morris's real offense here is calculation: he thinks so highly of himself and his abilities that he feels he ought to wait about the marriage, and not run the risk of marrying Catherine with only a third of her prospective income. In other words, Morris is greedy for money. This is understandable, in view of his lack of that necessary medium-but he is bargaining life itself away for the elusive prospect of more money, and for James, this is an offense against both life and love. If Morris cared that much for Catherine, he would marry her immediately.

SECTION XXIII

Mrs. Penniman is not invited on the European trip; in fact, the Doctor prefers that she not come, so he can separate Catherine from what he considers her unfortunate and indeed baleful influence. Mrs. Penniman rather spitefully calls Catherine's attention to what she believes is her father's purpose in the trip-to take Catherine out of sight, and therefore out of the mind, of Morris.

Catherine says that this is mistaken, and she arranges to meet Morris very shortly. Somehow, she hopes that he will ask her, in fact plead with her, to stay home. She will do whatever he requests. Morris asks her if she wouldn't like to see all of the wonderful works of art over in Europe, and when she says that she would not, she would prefer to be with him, he thinks to himself that she is a very dull person. Morris tells her that she ought to see Europe-it may mollify her father, so that he would be more agreeable to the marriage.

Catherine and her father go on the grand tour of Europe; they are gone not six, but twelve months, studying art and antiquity, while Mrs. Penniman remains at home, in the house at Washington Square, where Morris is her most frequent visitor. As the scene concludes here, Mrs. Almond discusses with her sister the question of Morris Townsend, and reproaches Lavinia Penniman for her ill judgment in bringing together the two, since she does not honestly think that Morris will be a good husband for Catherine. If he gets all of the money, perhaps he will be passable; otherwise, says Mrs. Almond, he will take a terrible revenge on her.

Comment

Here one sees additional motivation for Mrs. Penniman's actions. She has not minded Catherine's absence, and she enjoys inviting Morris to the house, presumably for refined conversation about his prospects. Morris acquiesces; the house, after all, is elegant, and he is poor, so that it becomes for him "a club with a single member." At this point, it appears that both Mrs. Penniman and Morris are regarded by James as essentially flawed characters, without the depth which will enable them to stick with anything. Catherine is more and more emerging as the soundest of the four principals, by contrast with them, though all of them reproach her for one reason or another - and that includes Morris.

SECTION XXIV

Dr. Sloper, as part of his plan for what amounts to the brain-washing of Catherine, does not mention their difference of opinion over Morris for the first six months they are abroad. She does not appear to be behaving as a victim, but the Doctor is still not sure of her, other than that he still thinks of her as very unintelligent and insensitive. Meanwhile, she does receive letters from Morris, but she will not pain her father by discussing them with him.

Then, at the mid-point of their European journey, one day in the Alps, he asks her the question: has she given [Morris] up? And the answer he gets is no, which causes him to say to her that he is very angry. But she has told the truth, as she always does-alone among the four principals, incidentally, for even the Doctor has been guilty of deception. Here he is most threatening; as threatening as anyone has been to her. He says that probably if she marries Morris, she will be left in a place somewhat like the deserted Alpine location and will starve of shift for herself. The Doctor speaks violently against Morris. Then the subject is abruptly dropped for six more months, to reappear at the very end of their European trip.

Again he asks her intentions. She says that when they return home, the marriage with Morris will probably take place. The Doctor is aghast, though he tries not to show this; he is cutting, and tells Catherine that she has now received a liberal education at his expense, from which Morris will benefit. "We have fattened the sheep for him before he kills it," says her father, and she stares blankly at him, with such a caustic statement before her for consideration.

Comment

Here the battle of wills continues. Dr. Sloper sees that he has made no impression against what he regards as Catherine's extreme stubbornness. Meanwhile, Catherine herself has been violent to her father in this scene; the first time this has been so. She defends Morris against her father's charge that he will let her starve. Here is a hint that the battle of wills is beginning to move toward its climax.

If this were an ordinary romance or love-story, we could predict the outcome; the Doctor would relent at the end, and love will find a way to unite Catherine and Morris. But this simply cannot be predicted in a work by James. Unlike his friend and contemporary William Dean Howells, who called for a portrayal of "smiling realism," James tries to show life as it really happens, and if he generally chooses a social stratum where the mere struggle for economic existence is not paramount, the struggle is still there, translated to a higher level: the struggle for life and freedom, and for that which makes life worth living at a higher level of awareness. And this is the real struggle in *Washington Square*.

SECTION XXV

Catherine sees Morris the day after she arrived in New York. Meanwhile she has spoken at great length about him to Mrs. Penniman. Morris had sat in her father's study upon occasion while they were away, and this makes Catherine unaccountably nervous. Also, it seems that Morris has found employment as a commission merchant-he is in partnership.

Now Catherine admits that the plan for her to talk her father around to the marriage in Europe had been Morris's, and that it had not worked. On the other hand, neither had that of her father's-to talk her out of marriage with Morris. She sternly tells her aunt that she has come home to be married, and that she will never plead for anything again to her father.

Mrs. Penniman is somewhat amazed, even frightened, at the new forcefulness of Catherine, and at the most authoritative speech she has ever heard from Catherine. So she cannot say anything in reply.

Comment

The suspense here is truly built up. Catherine, at any rate, has grown in dramatic, even tragic, stature. But we are still not sure of the reaction of her young man. Enough doubt about him has been planted in the mind of the reader by James that we just do not know how he will react.

SECTION XXVI

The meeting of Morris and Catherine, after a year of separation, occurs here. Morris sounds her out on the subject of whether her father has relented toward him, and is very disappointed, as he shows, upon learning that Dr. Sloper is as inflexible as ever. His pride is touched; he does not like to be beaten, any more than does the Doctor. Yet he expects to succeed in business. Meanwhile Catherine cannot make Morris understand how she feels, and why she will not ask her father for anything further-her father is simply not very fond of her, she tells Morris. We must not depend, or even seem to depend, on her father, she tells her lover further-she will accept nothing from him. And she extracts from Morris his promise never to despise her.

Comment

Now it is looking even more as though Morris will never get what he wants, if what he wants is the inheritance from Dr. Sloper should he marry Catherine. The process of seriously testing Morris and his love for Catherine herself, apart from her prospective fortune, is beginning in earnest. And we, the audience, still do not know for sure what will happen in this case.

SECTION XXVII

The Doctor notifies his sister, Lavinia, that as to Morris Townsend he has not budged an inch in his opinion. He is sure, without asking sordid questions, that Morris has been a guest in the house very frequently, and this is the only entertainment Morris may look for from the Doctor. But if Lavinia has encouraged Morris, she may look for him to take a revenge. Will Morris Townsend "hang on?" asks Dr. Sloper of his sister. Lavinia replies, hurt, that of course he will hang on. But the Doctor is not so sure.

Meanwhile, Lavinia Penniman is now in the midst of intrigue. She is in close touch with Morris, but the Doctor has rattled her with his suggestion that Morris may turn on her. She is afraid of Morris, suddenly. Morris is no longer deferential toward her; instead, he is rather brutal.

Comment

The relationships among the four principals are changing somewhat at this point. Catherine has become more decisive and more forceful. Morris is showing more of his innate weakness. Indeed, the mysteries of personality and motivation, which have been left in the dark by James are now gradually working themselves into the open, dramatically. We will soon see the resolution of the mystery, or so we might feel by various hints.

WASHINGTON SQUARE

··

SECTION XXVIII

Mrs. Penniman continues to correspond with Morris, telling him that the Doctor still hates him, and will not relent. Catherine, she adds, seems to be expecting to be married soon. Mrs. Penniman makes some helpful suggestions about an elopement, which Morris simply ignores.

Mrs. Penniman suggests, half jokingly and half naively, that Morris might bring a lawsuit against the Doctor. But his answer is that he is beaten – he knows that the Doctor will never change, and he therefore declares suddenly that he must give up Catherine. The action has been leading up to this remarkable statement; if Morris cannot have Catherine with her money, he will not have her at all. He is a most uncharacteristic and un-ardent lover, to think, much less to say, such things. The rationalization which Morris uses is this: "I can't bring myself to step in between her and her father-to give him the pretext he grasps at so eagerly (it's a hideous sight!) for depriving her of her rights."

Even here, Mrs. Penniman's fatal and near-comic weakness for romantic situations enters in; she will have a scene between Catherine and Morris arranged so that there can be a last parting. Morris is not planning on marriage with anyone else; he will instead, he says, do something "brilliant," perhaps in business. We are still not that sure about his abilities, but maybe he will succeed.

Comment

Here again we see Mrs. Penniman's dangerous tendency to play with lives, from which she aims to extract emotion. Morris wants to be finished with the whole relationship, and while he has talked himself into a noble and altruistic renunciation "for Catherine's sake," the truth seems to be that he is getting tired of Catherine even if he was at one time interested in her as a woman; he is more interested in money.

SECTION XXIX

Here occurs the parting and the break which has been led up to. Morris is very brutal toward Catherine. Perhaps even he has a bad conscience concerning his treatment of her, though this does not seem too possible. He asks her not to make a scene, as all women do - and he says that he is planning to go away for a while "on business." But, as Catherine says, his business is to be with her. At that he says that he does not earn his living with her, and that his reputation has been damaged already by the allegation that maybe he does; that he will allow himself to be kept at her expense. He talks rather vaguely of going to New Orleans to buy some cotton. There is a sudden fear which comes over Catherine, as though what she had imagined will now come to pass. She has given up everything for him. Now she sees that he will leave and not come back. But she must still follow the law of her own nature, which is not to allow him to take an unfair advantage of her or to make her plead with him, as she had done with her father.

Comment

With Morris's closing of the door, as he leaves the house, we have a rather good idea that the affair is over. He promises that she will see him again, but one is reluctant to believe him. But we knew that this would happen. Morris has gradually and dramatically been revealing his character, and now the story is complete about him, except for a form of postscript. He has been weak, and in a way the Doctor, by his treatment of Morris, had made a self-fulfilling prophecy about him.

SECTIONS XXI-XXIX

Catherine has been damaged in this section or group of sections of the work, first by her father, and then by Morris. But there has been a fatal inevitability about it all, which we have been expecting since the third unit of the work - and perhaps from its very start. There has been further suspense in this fourth unit; will Catherine remain true, and will Morris? James skillfully arouses some doubts about this, but it is interesting to observe, from the point of view of sheer fictional technique, how he treats Morris as compared with Catherine. We are sure of her fidelity and constancy, but are much less sure of Morris. And what is the source of these reservations?

For one thing, the sheer description of the actions and the bearing of Morris conveys more than a hint of effeteness, as against the Doctor's almost inhuman firmness. He is an idler, and he is indolent-but we suppose that perhaps Morris will come out all right, because that is the way romances always end. But *Washington Square*, though it deals with a frustrated love affair, is not a romantic novel at all; rather, it is a realistic work of art, perhaps approaching more the nature of tragedy than of romance. A woman is not considered by Aristotle, prime theoretician of tragedy, as the most admirable or appropriate subject for tragedy, and there is some question as to whether Catherine qualifies as such. But one thinks of the magnificent Greek tragedy, the *Antigone* of Sophocles, to see another such steadfast woman, accused of pride and of disobedience, persevering to the end.

Now, it cannot be said that Catherine Sloper is Antigone. But there are points of resemblance, or at least analogy. Catherine is a slighter creation, a slighter figure, than Antigone. And it can be objected that she remains, after all, very much alive, whereas that is not Antigone's fate; she dies, as punishment for having transgressed the law of Creon, Tyrant of Thebes. And this law she transgresses in conformity to a higher law. Her manner of death is to be shut up in a cave, still alive. Creon, for his treatment of her, amounting to impiety in the Greek view, loses both his son and his wife.

Now it is hard to know whether James had in mind such a thing as the use of the Antigone myth-legend. As we shall see in the final section of the story of *Washington Square*, the life left to Catherine is a stunted one; figuratively she is shut up in a cave.

But the point of this comparison is that it may be necessary to consider the work somewhat at the level of myth or legend in order to find out the ultimate meaning of *Washington Square*.

SECTION XXX

This was, James tells us, almost the last outbreak of passion in Catherine's life-a long and terrible outbreak. She expected Morris to return and knock at the door, but he did not do so. What especially concerned her was that her father should not see how she felt about this tremendous shock, so a half-hour after Morris's abrupt and indeed brutal departure, she appeared at the dinner table. Then she went to her own room; she could not face her father and aunt.

Mrs. Penniman comes and asks Catherine if she can do anything, but is told to leave her alone. Meanwhile Catherine, sitting up half the night, expected Morris to ring at the door. Mrs. Penniman suspected that Morris had left, but Catherine would not admit this.

Catherine dispatched notes to Morris, telling him that he was killing her-but no answers were forthcoming. Meanwhile the Doctor has figured out that "the scoundrel has backed out." Then Catherine goes out, and when she returns, Mrs. Penniman questions her. "We must study resignation," she says. Catherine admits that she had inquired at Morris's residence, and that she had been told that he had left town. And Catherine has a fair idea that Morris has been influenced by Mrs. Penniman. The latter admits this, in a way, and Catherine accuses her of being quite cruel.

Mrs. Penniman accuses Catherine of being an ungrateful girl. At the end of the scene, she says that Catherine was given up by Morris out of consideration for her, because he did not wish to injure Catherine in the eyes of her father and perhaps imperil her inheritance. As the scene ends, Catherine indicates that she doesn't believe the story.

Comment

Here the foiled passion of Catherine breaks into the open, but that is natural enough. She also sees that she has been used; used by all three of the other principals, each for his or her own purpose. In this scene, then Catherine fully realizes her plight.

SECTION XXXI

Mrs. Almond is the hostess at one of the Sunday evening dinners which the Doctor, Mrs. Penniman, and Catherine attend. Mrs. Almond says that she is delighted that the marriage will not take place, but all the same, "he ought to be horsewhipped." Mrs. Penniman's answer is that Morris's renunciation had been prompted by the very noblest motives: the desire not to impoverish Catherine. Mrs. Penniman gives Catherine some more advice: that she should tell her father that the affair is going on as usual, and admit nothing about the break-up. But she adds that Catherine should tell her father that she is planning to be married shortly. "So I am," said Catherine.

Two days later, Catherine receives a letter from Morris, mailed at Philadelphia. It is five pages long. Morris says that he had acted out of altruistic motives, not wishing to ruin

Catherine's prospects. He would never, he says, "interpose between her generous heart and her brilliant prospects and filial duties." She keeps the letter for many years, in fact, and after she gets over what James calls the bitterness of its meaning and the hollowness of its tone, she is able to admire the grace of its expression. By this is meant perhaps the summation of Morris's character: the style is the man, indeed, for Morris does have grace of manner and expression, though he does seem basically hollow.

Catherine still does not wish to appeal to the mercy or even the sympathy of her father. But soon afterwards occurs a brutal scene between them, although its severity is hidden by the usual tempered language. He asks her when his house will be empty, and informs her that when she goes, presumably to be married, her aunt will go with her. Catherine finally says that she has broken off her engagement, and that she has asked Morris to leave New York, which he has done for a long time. The Doctor seems perplexed, though the probability is that he understands well enough. At the very end, after he has said: "You are rather cruel, after encouraging him and playing with him for so long!," James adds that the Doctor had his revenge, after all.

Comment

What is meant here, of course, is ironic, for Catherine has not dismissed Morris; he has dismissed her. The Doctor's statement of the situation, turned around as it is, is very hard for Catherine to take, and we can surmise that she barely controls herself. The key to this section occurs in the last lines of the piece, with the interchange, crackling with suppressed emotional violence, between Catherine and Dr. Sloper.

SECTION XXXII

Catherine had, we know, been "deeply and incurably wounded," as James says. The Doctor never does discover the exact truth, though he pries in an effort to learn from Mrs. Penniman and even Morris's sister, Mrs. Montgomery. But he learns nothing, for Mrs. Almond has little knowledge of her brother's whereabouts; he seems to have absented himself to California. Catherine knows Mrs. Almond better; the latter has taken her up, but still Catherine will not confide in her about Morris.

Doctor Sloper keeps congratulating himself in his opinions; he had been right, he tells himself, in saving Catherine from an unhappy, indeed wretched, marriage. Mrs. Almond says that it is most likely that Morris got rid of Catherine, rather than the other way around, but the Doctor doesn't quite believe this. He tells himself further that now Catherine is "better." Possibly this is so, but it is, as Mrs. Almond suggests, out of numbness, not out of resolution. Several years follow, because in this section the time is made to pass quickly; Catherine has had several proposals, each for a marriage of convenience, "a marriage of reason," in one case with a widower with several children, and in another with a very eligible younger man. But Catherine is not interested, and now she has passed her thirtieth year and is becoming an old maid, as James says, though her father now prefers that she marry. He hopes that she will not be too fastidious: "I should like to see you an honest man's wife before I die," he says.

The natural question to ask, then, is: "what was wrong with Morris," if the Doctor is not becoming overly-fastidious, but instead is changing in the opposite direction. And this is involved with the meaning of the story of *Washington Square*. Catherine has become interested in such things as charities, hospitals, and aid societies, and she is tending toward a "mature and deliberate" spinsterhood.

Comment

There is, as the Section more than implies, something vital missing in Catherine's life, though she recognizes it as her duty to try to fill this void, which is the absence of love. By age forty, she is an old-fashioned person, or is so regarded, and she has rather conservative moral and social opinions and manners. Mrs. Penniman, though older than Catherine, becomes younger-appearing, and this fact is highly significant. In such a tangle of relations, one has a forerunner of the great and obscure work of James's maturity; such a work as *The Sacred Fount*, in which, as one character seems to be growing older and losing strength and energy, another grows, or seems to grow, correspondingly younger. This is the **theme** of vampirism. It is certainly present, although in somewhat less subtle form, in *Washington Square*.

SECTION XXXIII

The Doctor, at age sixty-eight, one day abruptly tells Catherine that he would like her to promise something: that she will not marry Morris Townsend after he, Dr. Sloper, is dead. Morris has still not made his fortune; he has married and apparently gotten rid of his wife somehow, so the Doctor says, and further, he is now in New York again.

Catherine says that she rarely thinks of Townsend. "Promise," says the Doctor. He is, he tells his daughter, altering his will. But she still does not promise. She will not be treated the way she fancies he has treated her before.

The only time a patient of the Doctor's is mentioned, other than members of his own family, is on the occasion which caused his death; he has gone to visit a patient who was confined in an insane asylum, and caught a bad cold. He takes to his sickbed, telling Catherine that he will not recover but that he hopes he will be well nursed anyway. But his hold on life was not firm enough, and he died after three weeks.

The "pay-off," if one can use this word, comes when the Doctor's will is read, and it turns out that he has cut the share of Catherine to a fifth of what he had originally intended to leave her. And the wording of the will is such that really she wouldn't have profited much more had she gone ahead and married Morris. For the change to his will, which was "of recent origin," said: "She is amply provided for from her mother's side, never having spent more than a fraction of her income from this source; so that her fortune is already more than sufficient to attract those unscrupulous adventurers whom she has given me reason to believe that she persists in regarding as an interesting class." This seems to be a public denunciation of Catherine, or at least an expression of no confidence. But Catherine says that she likes the provisions of the will very much, only she wishes that he had chosen his wording differently.

Comment

Catherine's refusal to promise not to marry Morris Townsend seems to have been the cause of the Doctor's changing his will. This was a mean trick for him to play on her, and it showed how essentially foolish she was in not following the desires of her heart toward Morris Townsend, whether or not Morris was worthy of her. Catherine, from a practical point of view, had little likelihood of marrying Morris or anyone else, at her age. What the Doctor wanted from her, by his request for her promise that she would not marry Morris, was complete and final submission to his obstinate will. But she is equally as determined that she would not give in, and four-fifths of her inheritance is perhaps a cheap price for her to pay.

SECTION XXXIV

Catherine remains in Washington Square except for a month at the beach in August each year. She will not hear of giving up the old house; she also stays with Mrs. Penniman, because there is an attachment, if only founded upon dislike, between them.

One day, Mrs. Penniman informs Catherine that she has seen Morris Townsend. Catherine is non-committal. "I hope he was well," she remarks. Catherine also says that she hopes he will not see her; she would rather not see him. This is unexpected, and Mrs. Penniman had not mentioned his name in that house for perhaps twenty years. But Catherine is reserved, still. He married in Europe, but his wife died. He has not been back to New York for ten years, until a few days ago. All these things, as Catherine hears them from Mrs. Penniman, do not impress her, or at least evoke no reaction. Finally she says that she would prefer if Mrs. Penniman does not mention that subject again. But she is trembling, and her heart is beating violently. And she bursts into tears, though she hides them from Mrs. Penniman.

Comment

Catherine is still capable of being moved from this ghostly presence out of the past, though her father had tried to kill all such emotions in her, and had just about succeeded, adding insult to injury with the wording of the will. But we know that Catherine now will meet Morris.

SECTION XXXV

Morris has sent Catherine a message, through Mrs. Penniman, who asks her if she would be spoken to once more about "He whom you once loved."

The message is simply that Morris wishes to see Catherine, and that if she knew his wishes, she would consent to see him. He is going away again, and he wishes to meet her as a friend, nothing more. Catherine seems hard, saying to Mrs. Penniman that she wishes to be left alone by Morris. But the doorbell rings and Morris stands outside. Mr. Morris Townsend enters, after perhaps a quarter of a century away from that place.

Catherine "would never have known him." He still has a fine presence. But she gives him no help. He was nothing to her. She does not think that he ought to have come. He wants to be friends again. Catherine will not allow it. "Please don't come again," she instructs him, not even sitting down.

"You treated me badly," says Catherine. Morris's answer is that he had not wished to rob her of her quiet life with her father. Morris knows the contents of the Doctor's will, no doubt through Mrs. Penniman, but he cannot very well admit this. So an impasse is reached between them. Catherine says that she had nothing to gain by marrying. She coldly bids Morris good-bye, and as he leaves he reproaches Mrs. Penniman for having suggested the visit in the first place.

As the last little violent scene ends, Catherine is sitting in the parlor, picking up her sewing; she had "seated herself with it again-for life, as it were."

Comment

Catherine, by now hardened as a result of the tampering and suffering she has undergone, gives Morris his final dismissal. The Doctor had done his work well; Catherine is the ultimate loser, because at one time she had been worth, at least ethically, more than all three of the other principals put together. But it is too late for anything to be done for her by way of recompense. She has chosen her way of life: despite the pressures on her, it was her own will which weakened, under the pressures applied, until she was almost literally "brainwashed" into another state of being.

And Morris? His life is no better. He and Catherine together could probably have had an adequate, and even a successful, marriage. But it was not to be, and in this, as has been pointed out, the story is a remarkably atypical one in the history of literature. Anyone familiar with the moral world in James's fiction can see that *Washington Square* is a characteristic work.

The vampiristic **theme** is a primary one, as is the theme of renunciation. But who renounces what? At the end, judging from the last two lines, Catherine has renounced life. Mrs. Penniman has never really lived, except vicariously-for many years. The Doctor is dead, but his malicious self-righteousness lives on to continue to do injury to Catherine. And Morris, who might in some way have benefited and developed if married to Catherine-he could hardly be worse now-is just a ruin. The tragedy of these blighted lives is complete.

SECTIONS XXX-XXXV

If these last sections are the last act of a tragedy, they are so by way of anticlimax, for nothing much seems to happen after Morris's violent dismissal of Catherine, and her painful waiting for him to return, which he refuses to do. The tragedy is more subtle, for it involves the murder of souls, not of bodies; Catherine has been so beaten about by Dr. Sloper that she has retreated and has been dulled in her moral perceptions. At the end of the work, Catherine is ethically on no higher a level than any of the other characters, and she demonstrates this by her behavior to Morris, who is really down and out.

Yet these last sections are absolutely necessary, for they are the proof of James's thematic interest. They are also very strange, that is if one persists in considering *Washington Square* a romance. If it is so, if it is "about" love, it proceeds to define what love is negatively.

The ending of the story, and of Catherine's real life, occurs at the end of Section XXIX, when Morris leaves the house. Until the very moment when this happens, we have not been absolutely sure that he would make such a break. If he had asked Catherine to go with him and marry him, she would at that point have done so. But the moment passed-it is almost Browning's doctrine of the infinite moment, in which the course of a life is set irrevocably. James does not cloud the issue: there is a measure of free choice here, on the parts of both Morris and Catherine, and the choice made is the wrong one, the evidence for which is found in the very last Section, when we see what has ultimately happened both to Morris and to Catherine.

WASHINGTON SQUARE

....

Doctor Austin Sloper

He seems outwardly a rather kindly man, successful in his noble profession of medicine, though having had more than his share of bad luck. He had lost both his beautiful young wife and his son, and was left, as a kind of consolation prize, with his daughter Catherine, whom he unconsciously contrasts unfavorably with his wife, who had the same name, to the detriment of his daughter. Dr. Sloper has been financially successful as well as professionally so; he might be described as a New York society doctor, with an earned income from his practice of at least twenty thousand dollars a year. Because he is temperate in his expenditure of money, his fortune has increased, and with the money which his wife had brought him as her dowry upon their marriage, he is a rather wealthy man.

One interesting thing about the sketch of Dr. Sloper provided by James is that the Doctor is almost never seen in the context of his profession. We see him only in his personal and family life. And as we get to know him better, through his dramatic self-revelation of character, we see some ugly things. He is so sure of his judgments and opinions that he ends up crushing his daughter's spirit, after having tampered with and violated it. Then he does a despicable thing when, upon his daughter's refusal to give in finally to his will and refuse to marry Morris Townsend after her father is dead - though it is many years after the original parting of Morris and Catherine - the Doctor practically cuts her out of his will. The Doctor has revealed what manner of man he is by his actions. He is an early edition of what was described in the essay above on James's Morality, the Jamesian Vampire. He is defined negatively, by what he dislikes: Morris Townsend, or the idea that Morris should presume to wish to marry his daughter. And the Doctor is quite self-deceived, believing as he does that he can judge what is best for his daughter, something that James always regarded with the deepest suspicion - the idea that one sovereign human personality can specify what is "best" for another.

Catherine Sloper

The Doctor's daughter, a rather charming and basically attractive girl, even if she is (at least in the Doctor's eyes) superficially plain. What happens to Catherine is most unfortunate, and though it is hedged with some humor, there are elements of tragedy in it because of the moral situation which is generated by her dilemma, brought about by the Doctor, to the effect that Catherine must choose between her duty to her father and her duty to her prospective husband. Catherine is pressured into making the wrong decision, and then punished rather diabolically by her father for doing what she thinks or is told is the right thing.

Catherine's character, under the stress of the complex situation, changes for the worse; she is an honest and trusting girl at the beginning, and at the end she is capable of a coldness almost equivalent to that demonstrated earlier by her father and then by Morris Townsend.

Morris Townsend

Catherine's lover. An idle young man, at least on the surface, who seems to have no great strength of character. He, too, is a victim of the Doctor; he is too weak to take the affirmative step of acting, rightly or wrongly, in the matter of his marriage to Catherine. Thus he delays until the psychological moment is past.

It is suggested by James that Morris's motives are so mixed and complex that perhaps even Morris is never sure just what part the property and the inheritance of Catherine play in his desire to marry her. Certainly these are an element of attraction for Morris. He finally sees that he will not obtain as much money with his wife as he would like, so the final break in Section XXIX occurs. But will Morris be a suitable husband for Catherine without the money? The **irony** is, from the point of view of the Doctor's attitude, that he probably would be. If he seems a little weak, he has some good qualities. His inability to succeed in business is after all no crime. But the Doctor's decision about him seems to be made on a very irrational basis, "upon liking," as it were. He does not like Morris, from their first meeting, and all else follows from this fact.

Morris never really recovers from the breakup of his romance. Though he leaves Catherine, for her own good as he tells himself and her, he is still deluding himself and postponing his life. Both Morris and Catherine may be said to have never lived, in that they delay living an independent life until it is much too late. Even Mrs. Penniman's fantasy-life, false as it is, seems to be better than that of Catherine and Morris, and James gives us a sign of this at the end when he says that Mrs. Penniman seems to have grown younger even as Catherine aged. This is not literally true, of course, but it is true from the point of view of the Jamesian moral vision.

Mrs. Penniman (Lavinia Sloper Penniman)

She is Doctor Sloper's older sister, who had made a marriage with an impecunious clergyman of whom her family did not approve, and ever since age thirty-three has been a widow living on her brother's charity. Periodically she is threatened with being ousted from the house on Washington Square.

Lavinia - and her name is significant as conjuring up a vision of the faded-roses-kind-of-gentility - is incurably romantic. We would say today probably that she is a frustrated woman. Since her own independent life has ended before it had fairly begun, and since she has no children, she lives vicariously through her informal job of bringing up the motherless girl, Catherine. She is a born intriguer; she thinks an elopement, a secret marriage, a marriage in defiance of parental wishes, a romantic thing and helps to promote it, even while jeopardizing her own security. Probably she lacks common sense. The prospective marriage might have prospered had she not been Catherine's friend and supporter; this on the basis that one can defend oneself from enemies if only his or her friends will not intervene. Essentially Mrs. Penniman feeds on the emotional situation. She, like Dr. Sloper, is a Jamesian vampire, but of a less subtle sort - for she does show poor judgment on a number of occasions, and she is infatuated with Morris herself, or not so much with Morris, but with the idea of being infatuated with and being paid court by a handsome younger man. If Lavinia is a fool, it still is true that she has the best part of the bargain, over a long period of time, and she does not suffer as does Catherine or Morris or even her brother, Dr. Sloper.

Washington Square As A Major Character

It may sound odd, but the Square itself is not only the titular being or entity of the novel, it is also a kind of character whose felt presence remains, and students or readers considering this book seriously might wish to see just how the atmosphere and setting furnished by Washington Square at the specific era described by James operates in the work. Many of James's studies of the conflict among subtle characters, in his role as what Joseph Conrad called "a historian of fine consciences," are given their titles from places, not characters. We may be looking at the story here in a way which James did not intend, but as observed earlier, part of the great popularity of this story stems from James's setting it in the atmosphere of what was even in the earlier nineteenth century the greatest city in the Western Hemisphere and one of the great cities of the world, East or West.

MINOR CHARACTERS

Mrs. Almond

She is the younger sister of Dr. Sloper, happily married, and possessing much more common sense and acumen than her widowed sister, Mrs. Penniman. She has married advantageously, and seems an attractive character, but she is not really a participant in the action, but rather a spectator or commentator, as when she says of Morris that he ought to be horsewhipped for deserting Catherine. Mrs. Almond, along with Mrs. Montgomery, seems a center of normality in this strange jungle of emotional combat.

Mrs. Montgomery

The sister of Morris Townsend. Also an admirable character, having very modest financial means, no husband, and five children to support. She has been widowed also, like Mrs. Penniman, but in a way she contrasts favorably with the latter, as she attends to her duty and even tries to help out her brother, of whose virtues and faults she has a balanced view.

Marian Townsend

Mrs. Almond's daughter, the cousin of Catherine, who is engaged to and who marries Arthur Townsend, a distant cousin of Morris.

John Ludlow

He does not even appear in the story, but is briefly described at the end as a younger man who was quite eligible and who proposed marriage to Catherine many years after her parting with Morris; he was refused by her.

Mr. Macalister

A widower with three children and a handsome fortune who also proposes to Catherine and is also refused; both of these proposals take place when Catherine is beyond her thirtieth year, and the Doctor has no particular objection to either suitor.

WASHINGTON SQUARE

. . . .

Question: What is the fictional technique principally employed in *Washington Square*?

Answer: The technique used in this work, which of course belongs to the earlier period of James's fiction, is that of the Omniscient Narrator. This is not at all the stream-of-consciousness technique as practiced, for example, by Faulkner in *The Sound and the Fury* or Joyce in *Ulysses*. Instead, what it implies is the existence of a consciousness, distinct from that of the author on the one hand (though actually his) and the characters on the other hand, which can see and describe the actions of all the characters in the story. This method is the oldest way of telling a story. It is historical rather than psychological, and it does not probe into the unconscious or subconscious mind in the same way as the stream-of-consciousness method does. The Omniscient Narrative can be used to good advantage where there are several very important characters in a story who interact without having much knowledge of each other's thoughts or motives; it is a dramatic method, and this is the case of *Washington Square*. In that work, the story is not told from the point of view of Catherine, or of Dr. Sloper, or of Mrs. Penniman, or of Morris Townsend; rather, it is told from the point of view of a consciousness which knows at least the external actions, and to a limited extent the thoughts, of all of the characters in the work, and this is the narrator-author, to whom we must attribute a degree of knowledge which ordinarily nobody could have, because it is so complete.

Question: In terms of James's ethical vision, which of the principal characters in *Washington Square* is the worst?

Answer: The answer to this seems rather clear-cut; it is Dr. Sloper, who has the greatest moral pretensions and therefore correspondingly the worst villainy, in part because of his self-deception. He ruins his daughter's only real prospects for an even minimally satisfactory marriage, and then he dares to go a step farther, which is really his offense par excellence, and cut her out of his will in exactly the way he had apparently threatened to do if she had married Morris Townsend.

The Doctor makes what for James is the fatal presumption: he knows, so he thinks, what is "best" for another sovereign human personality, and by conducting his life on such a principle he fails not only as a father but also as a human being. In the Jamesian moral world, it is perceived as almost impossible for one consciousness to give another any meaningful "advice"; this is seen as early as James's first novel, *Watch and Ward* (1871). Dr. Sloper, by concluding that Morris is a fortune-hunter (which he may be - that is not the point) ruins Catherine's life. For, James seems to be saying, even if the Doctor was absolutely right about Morris Townsend, he should have permitted Catherine to find this out for herself, because this is the only way that a person can flourish and develop. Compulsion and prohibition, of the kind used by the Doctor, cannot in James's view ever have any good result.

Question: Discuss the Jamesian **theme** of vampirism in *Washington Square*.

Answer: This novel belongs to James's early period of literary development, and therefore the **theme** of vampirism is not developed in it with quite the subtlety which is seen in later works, especially the great works of James's maturity such as *The Golden Bowl* and *The Wings of the Dove*. But it is definitely present in more than rudimentary form, for if it were not, *Washington Square* would not be readable on any level beyond that of simply a good story.

The Doctor is the primary Jamesian vampire, and Mrs. Penniman is the secondary such character in *Washington Square*. There are degrees of guilt between the two, because it is clear that the Doctor is much more in a position to know what he is doing than is the much shallower Mrs. Penniman. Essentially, though, the offense of both of these characters against Catherine is one against the sovereignty of her personality. Both of them feed on Catherine, and thereby gain support for their own lives. While we do not see the Doctor in his public or professional life, we do seem to have here a man whose life is given up to a negative passion: to prevent, for what seems no particularly good reason, someone from doing something, rather than to encourage some more positive action or relationship. This, in James's moral world, is always an evil. The Doctor seems to have won, because in the process of revenge, he has escaped what Catherine might do if he had still been alive when the will is revealed and it turns out that Catherine has practically nothing from him, nor can she revenge herself-for by now she is so cheapened and corrupted in character that she welcomes revenge. On the other hand, Mrs. Penniman is a less serious, more sentimental, vampire. She does draw on Catherine's vitality, by vicariously enacting the love-affair with Morris Townsend, but her motivations are more understandable and less vicious than the Doctor's.

Question: Is Morris Townsend a fit husband for Catherine, or is he as bad as Doctor Sloper assumes he is?

Answer: It is probable that James meant to imply that the marriage should, for Catherine's sake, have taken place. Morris is weak, and of course the money and property play a certain part in his desire for Catherine. But this is not the same thing as saying that his only motive is the desire for money. He does rationalize about Catherine, and it turns out that much of what the Doctor thinks about him is true. But it is the Doctor who in part makes Morris weak. Morris's sister, Mrs. Montgomery, sees rather clearly that the marriage would not be good for Morris, if he were to have for a father-in-law such a person as the Doctor, and this is why she cautions Dr. Sloper not to let Morris marry his daughter.

Morris Townsend is indeed the best marriage possibility whom Catherine has encountered, and if his motives are mixed and ambiguous, so, James implies, are most motives. And even if the very worst had happened, and the marriage had been an outrageous failure, at least Catherine and Morris would have had their freely-chosen chance for life, which they rejected out of inertia and out of the pressures imposed upon them by the Doctor. Morris is unformed and neutral; it is only under the stress of his situation that he behaves viciously toward Catherine during the parting scene in Section XXIX, and then he has been driven to this step, and rationalizes it to the point that he thinks he is doing Catherine a favor, in helping her to protect her inheritance - though this is, ironically, not even the case as the Doctor changes his will anyway.

Question: How is Washington Square itself a kind of character in this novel?

Answer: The answer lies in the presence of this highly specific and solid place, representing as it does a way of life of a particular location and era and city. Washington Square forms the lives of those who live therein, and this in part accounts for the title. It is a settled life, at least on the surface, and a life with the expectation of comfort if not of the very greatest wealth and fortune.

Part of the effect of this novel lies in its contrast between the surface placidity and the troubled depths of the action. The novel does outline a conflict which results in the wrecking of several lives. Therefore, it can be said that there is violence in it, but it is a hidden violence, as is so often the case in James's work.

The situation is as though James had, while a young man seeing the fine houses in Washington Square (and more than likely, this happened), imagined what might have been going on in the personal lives of the people dwelling therein.

The novel gives a picture of the City, incidentally, which has been of key importance in making this not only one of James's most readable works, but one of his most popular ones, overseas as well as in the United States.

HENRY JAMES

There are no really significant separate studies of *Washington Square,* other than perhaps the Preface to the Dell Laurel Edition by R. P. Blackmur previously cited. The key to further research on *Washington Square,* in the opinion of the present author, lies in the study of the relation of that work to the theme of vampirism, as discussed in the section on James's Morality, above.

Oscar Cargill's *The Novels of Henry James* (New York: Macmillan, 1961), while rather neglecting a detailed account of *Washington Square* in favor of what are generally considered the more major novels of James, can provide a valuable overview of Jamesian fiction for the student.

Since there is so much that has been written on James, the student must have some principle of selection. This can be accommodated under the headings of Biography, Criticism, and Bibliography. Consultation of the following works, at a minimum, will at least insure that the student will read a good selection of the better and more useful articles and books bearing on James in general and on the particular works of James.

BIOGRAPHY

The best place to begin on the biography of Henry James is his own works: *A Small Boy and Others*, 1913; *Notes of a Son and Brother*, 1914; and *The Middle Years*; 1917. These three volumes, which contain many important reflections by James on his family and personal life, are edited in one volume by F. W. Dupee, *Henry James's Autobiography*, 1956.

The outstanding biography of Henry James, and an outstanding biography in itself, is written by Leon Edel, who reconstructs the life of James from all possible sources, especially from his letters. The biography will be in four volumes when it is completed. At the present, three volumes have appeared: *Henry James: The Untried Years, 1843-1870*, 1953; *Henry James: The Conquest of London, 1870-1881*, and *Henry James: The Middle Years, 1882-1895*, both in 1962. The fourth volume, *The Master, 1895-1916*, is in preparation.

An excellent one-volume study of James with very sound criticism throughout and an excellent view of James's career is F. W. Dupee's *Henry James*, 1951.

Of importance in studying James fully are his letters: *Selected Letters of Henry James,* edited by Leon Edel, 1960.

CRITICISM

All James students should begin with two edited works of James's own writings, for they contain extraordinary insight into the problems that he faced as a writer and a critic. James's methods of writing and making notes can best be seen in *The Notebooks of Henry James,* edited by F. O. Matthiessen and Kenneth Murdock, 1947. James's "Prefaces" are collected in a separate volume by

R. P. Blackmur, who supplies an excellent introduction with an analysis of the subjects of the prefaces and their general ideas. The volume is published as *The Art of the Novel*, 1959.

All the literary histories of American literature contain chapters on Henry James, and a beginning student will do well to begin with one of these. A long chapter by R. P. Blackmur on James in the *Literary History of the United States*, 1948, gives a complete view of James.

Of the separate volumes on James, a very useful one for the student is a collection of essays edited by F. W. Dupee, *The Question of Henry James*, 1945. There are discussions and essays by different critics on most of the problems in James study.

One early study, which was particularly critical of James's expatriation to Europe and questioned the whole idea of Europe because it was seen too idealistically by the later James, was, Van Wyck Brooks's *The Pilgrimage of Henry James*, 1925.

A very detailed, though somewhat dated, and excellent analysis of the backgrounds and the significance of James' style is done by Joseph Warren Beach, *The Method of Henry James*, 1918.

A short and general view of the whole subject, very valuable to the beginning student, is Leon Edel's *Henry James*, 1960, University of Minnesota Pamphlets on American Writers.

BIBLIOGRAPHY

Almost all of the above works have useful bibliographies for the beginning student. These in turn will lead on to other studies on Henry James.

A good descriptive bibliography, that organizes the criticism of James in order for the student, is the one by Robert E. Spiller in *Eight American Authors: A Review of Research and Criticism,* edited by Floyd Stovall, 1956.

A much fuller bibliography is Leon Edel's and D. H. Laurence's *A Bibliography of Henry James*, 1958.

Lightning Source UK Ltd.
Milton Keynes UK
UKHW020643020322
399449UK00009B/496